The ethos of beer is
share what you have.

– John Stoner

Table of Contents

Beer Basics

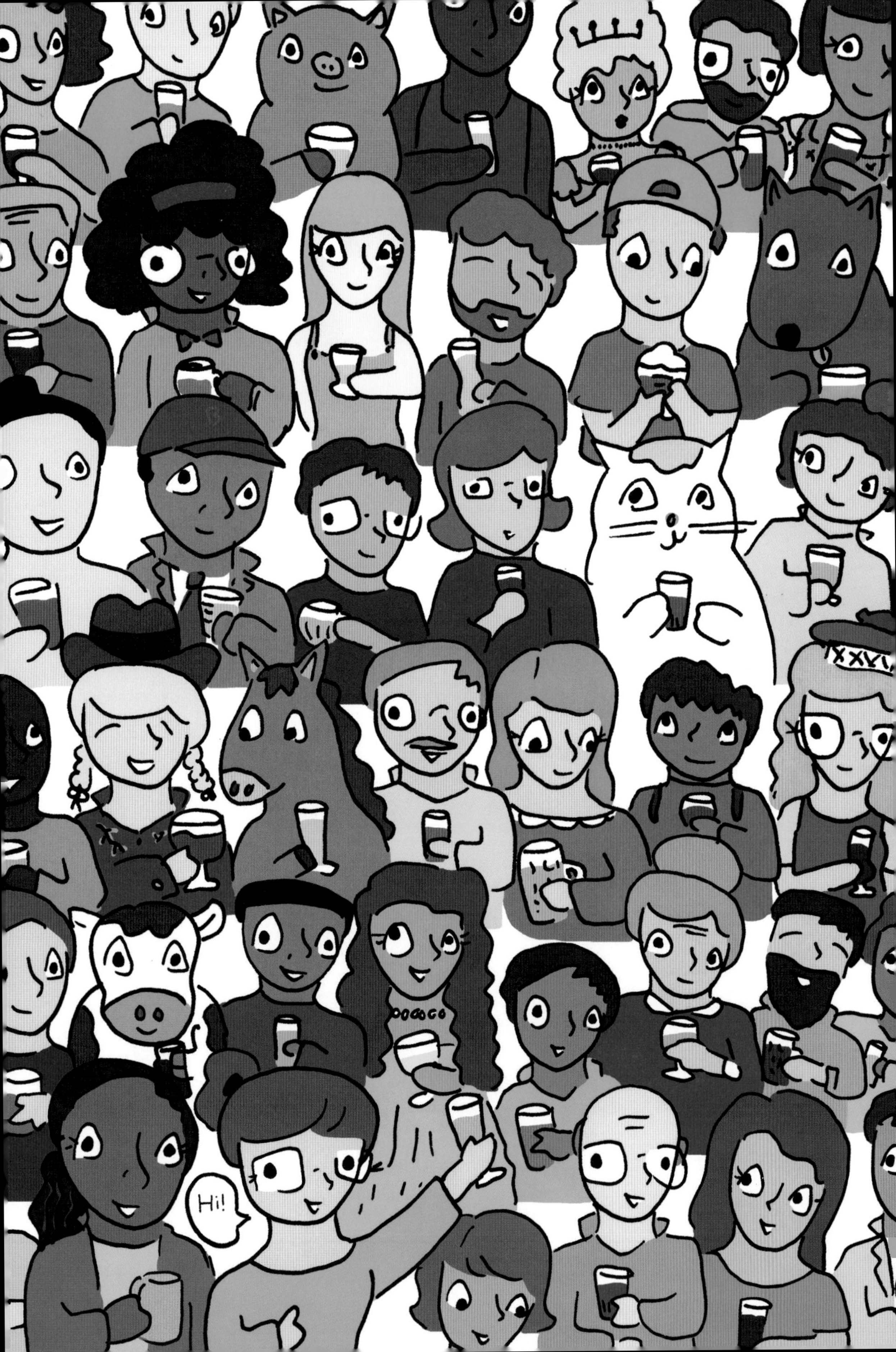
Hi!

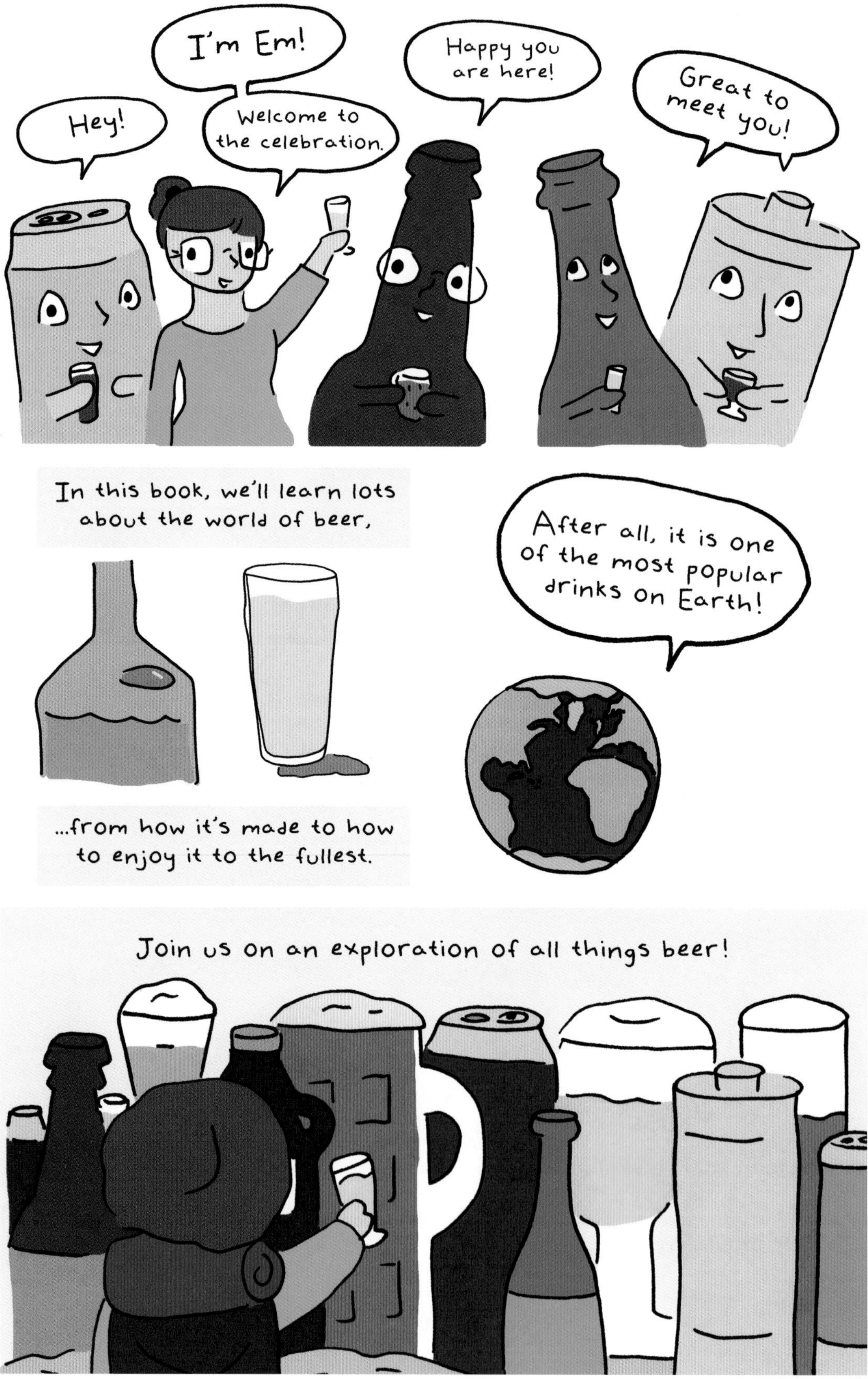
Hey!
I'm Em!
Welcome to the celebration.
Happy you are here!
Great to meet you!
In this book, we'll learn lots about the world of beer,
...from how it's made to how to enjoy it to the fullest.
After all, it is one of the most popular drinks on Earth!
Join us on an exploration of all things beer!

I don't think it would be right to start this book without a beer in our hands. Let's taste!

What do you see? Is the beer hazy? Clear? Does it have good foam? What color is the beer?

Swirl the glass counterclockwise; release those aromatics!

Drive-by: This is where you pass it under your nose quickly and take a sniff. What do you smell?

Now take a short sniff. Look for hop, malt, and yeast aromatics as well as off-flavors.

Take another, longer sniff. Notice anything different?

Now take a sip and let the beer warm up inside of your mouth before swallowing. Do you taste the hops, malt, water, or yeast?

Swallow and exhale through your nose. Notice any different aromas?

It's just that easy to get the most out of beer. Cheers!

What is Beer?

The four main ingredients in beer are:

water

malt

hops

yeast

Beer is like music—only a certain amount of notes, but a world of sound.

Lighter malts create flavors of cracker and grain, while dark malts taste like chocolate or coffee.

Different hops have different flavors, which can take beers like IPAs to a whole new level.

Certain yeast strains create flavors of clove, banana, white pepper, pear, apple—even barnyard (yes, barnyard!).

And even water can add salinity, create fuller or crisper mouthfeel, and accentuate dryness.

Through science and culinary skill—and a little magic—malt, hops, yeast, and water create the basis of something truly extraordinary.

How To Pour Beer!

Pouring beer is easy to master once you learn the steps.

Tip glass 45 degrees

Pour down side until half full

Turn glass straight

Finish pouring

Most beer should have an inch or so of head

Drinking and driving is a dangerous combo!

Driving under the influence is dangerous and illegal!

Drinking too much also makes you feel lousy.

When out drinking, assign a designated driver.

And just be smart!

Beer History

Alcohol has been an important part of civilization since Stone Age people enjoyed fermenting fruit or honey in primitive vessels.

We party tonight!

One of the first fermented drinks was discovered in Jiahu, China.

Pottery shards had remnants of a 9,000-year-old beverage made of rice, grapes, and honey.

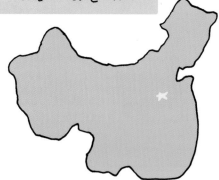

The Chinese developed pottery 5,000 years before any other civilization!

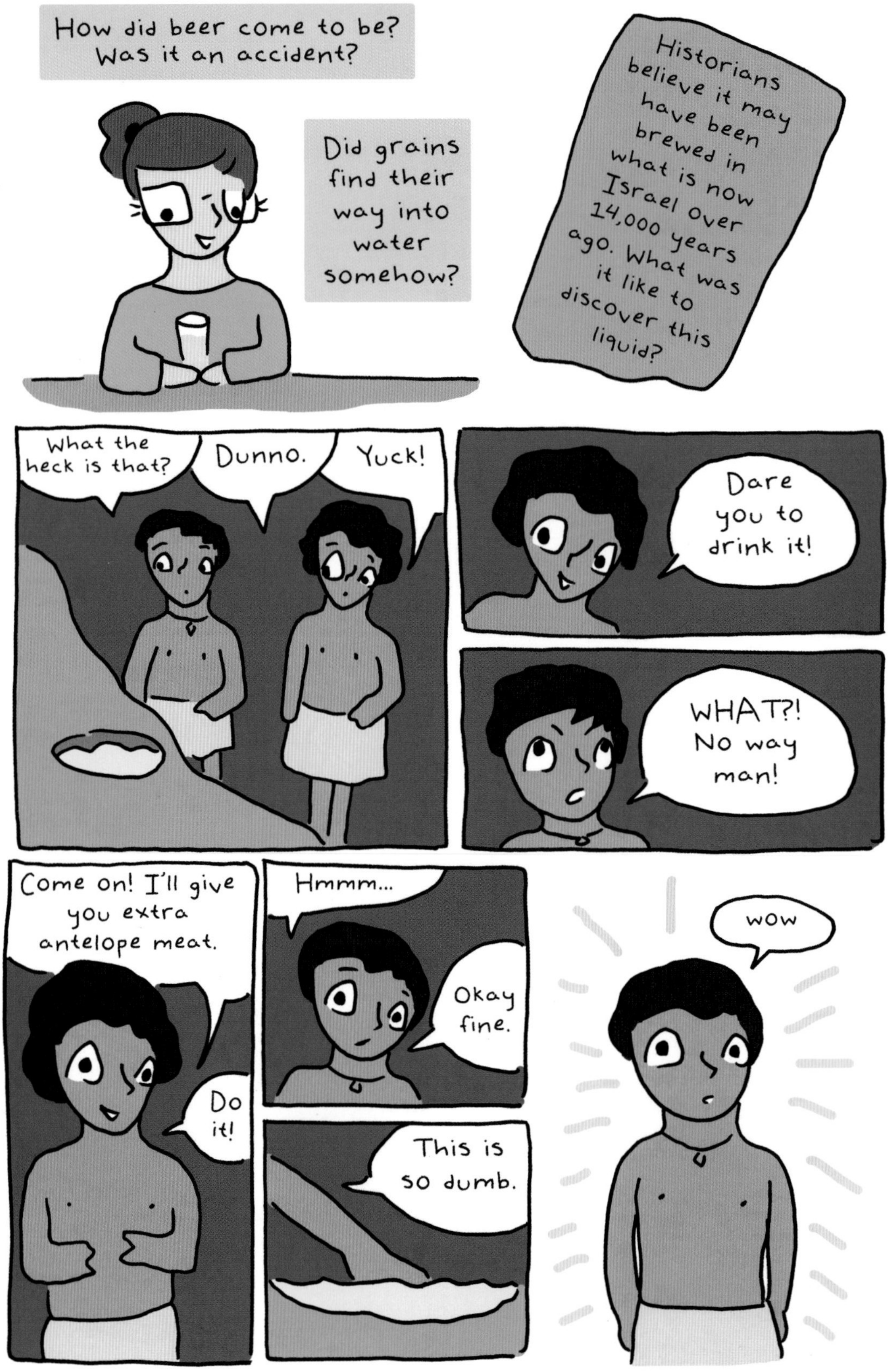
How did beer come to be? Was it an accident?
Did grains find their way into water somehow?
Historians believe it may have been brewed in what is now Israel over 14,000 years ago. What was it like to discover this liquid?
What the heck is that?
Dunno.
Yuck!
Dare you to drink it!
WHAT?! No way man!
Come on! I'll give you extra antelope meat.
Do it!
Hmmm...
Okay fine.
This is so dumb.
wow

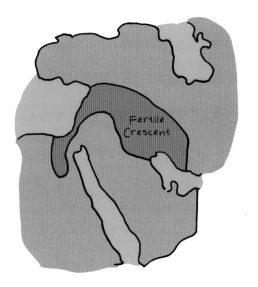

The first beer culture was in the Fertile Crescent, known now as the Middle East, where domestic grains and farming became popular around 9,000 B.C.

People around this time stopped being nomads and grew grain that could be made into beer, bread, and other staples.

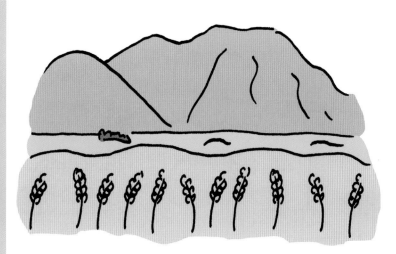

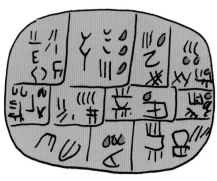

Cuneiform tablet

By 3,000 B.C. the Sumerians praised a goddess of beer, drank in taverns, and had written beer recipes and laws for the taxation of alcohol.

In Ancient Egypt beers were part of daily life.

Cross-section of an Egyptian beer vessel

Straws were used to filter out unwanted sediment!

They used a wide variety of ingredients in their beers:

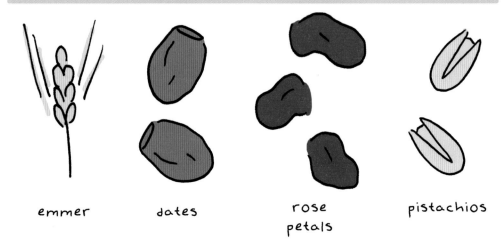

emmer

dates

rose petals

pistachios

Egyptians also had divine beings dedicated to beer:

Hathor: Goddess of love, and mistress of drunkenness!

Bes: God of the home and patron of brewers.

Other ancient cultures loved beer!

The Irish Celts

The Picts

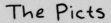

The Gauls

The Vikings

Ancient beers were spiced with a variety of plants. Some of those (like henbane) could be psychotropic.

henbane

Far out man!

The word "beer" comes from the Latin bibere which means "to drink."

Roman soldiers enjoyed beer when stationed in what is now northern England.

Beer was very important to our ancestors.

Pharaohs were buried with thousands of beer jugs to sustain themselves in the afterlife!

Beer was used in ceremonies...

Great job!

Building pyramids is my life.

...and it was used as payment.

Beer was also a great source of nutrition:

It provided hydration

It contained vitamins

And it had calories for energy!

Let's hear it for the ladies! Women were the main brewers/bakers throughout most of history until the Industrial Revolution in the 18th century.

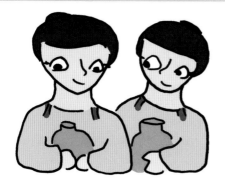

China

Mesopotamia

Egypt

Sub-Saharan Africa

Pre-Columbian Americas

Medieval European Alewives

What was beer like before hops were used?

In medieval Europe, hops were not widely used in brewing. Instead, there was "gruit"—a blend of herbs and spices used as a flavoring and preservative.

Gruit was a secret blend sold by the church or other governing body.

Use of gruit was MANDATORY. This was a way to collect taxes on beer and brewing.

No one really knows for sure what was in gruit since it changed by season. Each region had its own blend. Some common ingredients were...

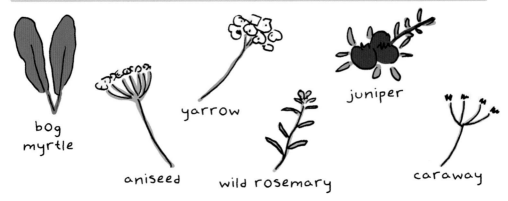

bog myrtle

aniseed

yarrow

wild rosemary

juniper

caraway

Hops were used in beer starting in the Middle Ages.

St. Hildegarde, who was a playwright, composer, and mystic also wrote about hops in beer in the 1150s.

as a result of its own bitterness it keeps some putrefactions from drinks, to which it may be added, so that they may last so much longer

Hops had become popular and were widely used in Europe by the 15th century.

Beer became big business in the 18th century with the first mass-produced beer, porter!

The Industrial Revolution propelled porter into a big, big business. It was named for the porters of London, who really enjoyed this style of beer.

Millions of barrels of porter were brewed, prompting larger and larger wood vessels to store and mature them in. These could be more than 750,000 U.S. gallons in size.

For scale, an Olympic swimming pool is 660,000 U.S. gallons of water!

Porter goes international! Colonialism and export sales drive new styles.

Baltic porter

Export stout

Imperial stout

Pre-Prohibition porter

Porter was important to British colonists in America.

pumpkin

molasses

walnut shells

Americans used ingredients they found in the New World to create their brand of porter.

America's founding fathers were HUGE fans of porter.

Stronger porters were shipped to Russia, where they were drunk by Catherine the Great and her imperial court.

Technological Advances in Brewing

Thermometer

Invented in the early 18th century. This changed almost every aspect of brewing, from boiling to fermentation.

Hydrometer

Measures the amount of dissolved sugars in wort (unfermented beer). This helped brewers calculate efficiency and ABV.

Drum Roaster

Patented by Daniel Wheeler in the early 19th century. This created black malts that made brewing dark beers more economical and consistent.

Refrigeration

Refrigeration started to show up in breweries in the 1870s. By the end of the 19th century, refrigeration of packaged beer and fermentation vessels was common.

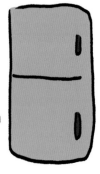

Emil C. Hansen isolated the first beer yeast strain in 1883.

Yeast

Louis Pasteur wrote important literature about yeast in the mid-19th century.

History of India Pale Ale

London brewers and ship captains partnered to bring beer to homesick Britons in India.

This beer was also made in cities like Burton-on-Trent.

The beer matured well on the ships and arrived in India in a sparkling, hoppy condition.

India pale ales became popular in England in the 1840s.

Plzeň, Czech Republic, 1842—The First Pilsner

The town's beer needed a makeover.

sigh

sigh

So Plzeň hired a German named Josef Groll to brew for them and hired Martin Steltzer to design a state of the art brewery.

Groll

Steltzer

Groll looked at the ingredients available to him and brewed a brand new style unseen before.

Very soft water

Floor-malted Moravian barley

Saaz hops

Lager yeast

The town got to try their new beer in the fall of 1842 at the St. Martin's Fair. It was very popular. That beer spawned countless copies throughout Europe.

19th-century American beer was an immigrant story.

The influx of German immigrants in the 19th century brought lager into the U.S. mainstream.

Bringing their brewing traditions and using American ingredients, many tasty beer styles were born in the 1800s.

California common

American pilsner

Cream ale

Beer also became regional! California (California common), Louisville, KY (Kentucky common), and the Rust Belt of Ohio/New York (cream ale) had beer styles unique to their areas.

PROHIBITION

We're going to skip this part, thanks.

No, you gotta talk about it!

But it's so sad! Okay, fine.

From 1920-1933, it was illegal to produce intoxicating beverages over 0.5%. Many breweries closed.

Beer was dumped all over the country. Many tears were shed in America when beer disappeared.

WAIL

All that beer!

Prohibition ended in 1933, to much delight!

WE WANT BEER
WE WANT BEER
WE WANT BEER

After Prohibition, breweries in America got much, much larger!

Nearly all beer produced was pale American lager.

Number of brewing companies in the U.S., 1909–1979

1622

44!

1909   prohibition   1979

But there was hope yet for beer lovers in America!

In the late 1970s President Jimmy Carter signed a bill legalizing homebrewing.

This is fun!

Homebrewing created a new generation of beer geeks.

Many were modeled after British pubs and served pub fare.

The 80s and 90s saw the rise of the brewpub.

A LOT of beer styles were created in the late 20th century!

Just to name a few!

American Wheat Beer

American IPA

Pumpkin Ale

Wheatwine

American Amber Ale

Imported beers and beers discovered on European trips also helped fuel the beer boom.

Selection at grocery stores also grew to include new brands.

In the 2000s, the buy local movement helped grow interest in local products. Breweries popped up everywhere.

Most Americans live within 10 miles of a craft brewery. That means almost anywhere you go, beer will be there!

What does the future hold for beer? Who knows!

Category 33: Best Brewery on Jupiter

And the winner is...

Celebrate Beer Pioneers

<u>Jack McAuliffe</u>
Co-owner of New Albion, the first microbrewery in America.

<u>Carol Stoudt</u>
One of the first female brewery owners/brewmasters and founder of Stoudt's Brewing Company.

<u>Michael Jackson</u>
British beer writer and author who championed Belgian beers.

<u>Ken Grossman</u>
Founder of Sierra Nevada, one of the largest craft breweries in America.

<u>Garrett Oliver</u>
One of the first Black brewmasters in America and celebrated author.

<u>Charlie Papizian</u>
Co-founder of the American Homebrewers Association® and Brewers Association.

Celebrate Beer Pioneers

Bert Grant
Founded the first modern brewpub in the United States in 1982.

Annie Johnson
First Black person to win Homebrewer of the Year at the National Homebrew Competition.

Charlie Bamforth
Former chair of Brewing Science at UC Davis and author of many technical brewing books.

Kim Jordan
Co-founder and former CEO of New Belgium Brewing.

Teri Fahrendorf
One of the first female brewmasters and founder of Pink Boots Society.

Fritz Maytag
Revived Anchor Brewing, one of the first national microbreweries.

The Brewing Process

I love to go to breweries to see the brewers and employees abuzz with activities.

But what is all this equipment? What does it do and how is it used to make delicious beers?

And what ingredients are used to make your favorite beer?

Let's have ourselves a little tour and do some exploring!

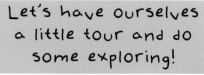

How Grains Become Your Favorite Beer: Hot Side

Hot side refers to heating the grains and water plus the straining and boiling of wort—the sugary liquid that will turn into beer.

Milling

Mash tun

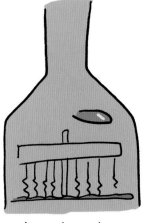

Lauter tun

Boil kettle

Whirlpool

How Grains Become Your Favorite Beer: Cold Side

Cold side refers to the cooling, fermentation, and packaging steps, which are all for the most part "cold" activities.

Heat exchanger

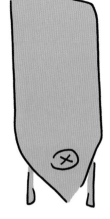

Fermentation tank

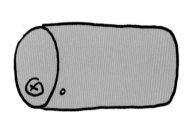

Maturation tank

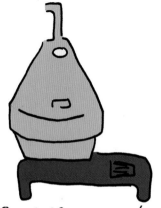

Centrifuge and/or filtration

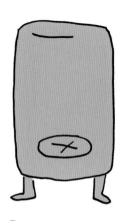

Bright tank

Packaging

Milling

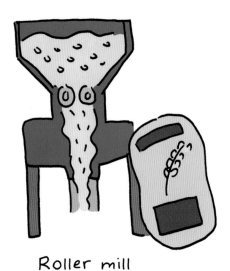

Roller mill

Grains like malt are milled to crack the outer husks and expose the sugars inside. Milling is a delicate art. Grind too finely and you can create issues; grind too coarsely and you won't be able to extract all the sugars you need to make beer!

Mashing

Mixed with hot water, enzymes from cracked malt convert starches into fermentable sugars through a process called mashing. The liquid (now called "wort") is allowed to simmer for approx. 60 minutes at a set temperature. Using a set temperature is an "infusion mash." There are other mashing techniques that vary in time and temperature, but this is the most popular mashing technique in American brewing.

Mash tun

Lautering

Lauter tun

The mash is put into the lauter tun, which acts as a sieve. Wort falls through the slotted floor, leaving the grain above; this separation is lautering. Liquid falls below the slotted floor, leaving the husks above. Rakes push the husks around the floor and hot water is sprinkled from above to try to get all available sugars out of the malt. This sprinkling is called "sparging."

Boiling

The wort is now boiled, usually for 60 to 90 minutes. Boiling sterilizes the wort. It also helps darken the beer and removes unwanted proteins and off-flavors.

Hops can be added at this stage. Hops added earlier add more bitterness than hops added later in the boil, which add more aroma. Certain beer styles require spices, which are usually added at the end of the boil.

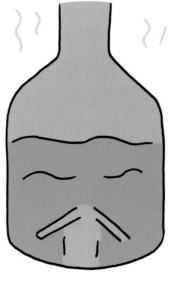

Boil kettle

Whirlpool

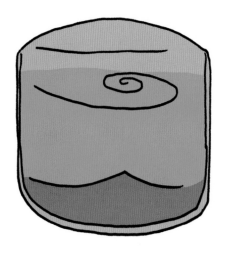

Whirlpool

In the whirlpool, centripetal forces help precipitate out unwanted proteins, hop particulates, and any other unwanted items. Hops can also be added during the whirlpool stage—these hops will contribute more flavor/aroma than being boiled since these attributes won't be boiled away or volatilized. The beer also has a chance to cool down slightly here.

Cooling

Beer needs to be cooled quickly in order for yeast to be pitched at the correct fermentation temperature. Hot wort is run through a heat exchanger where cool water runs next to it, cooling it down. Some beer styles like Belgian lambics are cooled the old fashioned way in a large metal open vessel called a "coolship." These beers don't need to be cooled quickly because they are inoculated with yeast from the air.

Heat Exchanger

Coolship

Fermentation

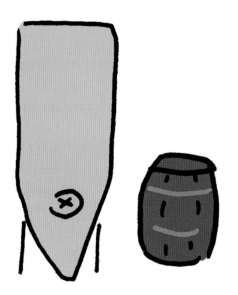

Fermentation usually takes place in stainless steel conical fermentors. Primary fermentation takes less than two weeks to complete for ales and lagers. Oak was traditionally the fermentation vessel material of choice and it is still used for Belgian sour beer production.

Maturation

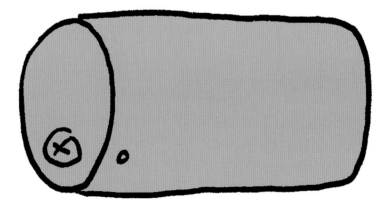

Lagers go through a much longer maturation process than ales, sitting at near freezing temperatures for weeks to months. This is the process of "lagering." Typically, lager tanks are horizontal to minimize pressure on the yeast.

Clarification

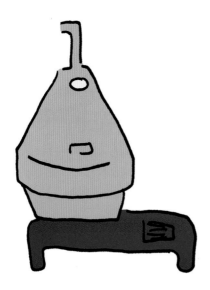

In larger breweries, filtration can be done using centripetal force to remove excess yeast and protein, rendering beer clear and shelf stable. This machine is called a centrifuge. Smaller breweries either use time, plate and frame filters, or other methods to clarify their beers.

Bright Tank

Before the beer is packaged, the beer is put into a tank called a bright tank (also called a "brite" tank). The beer is usually force carbonated here using a carbonation stone and also tested by the brewery staff or dedicated quality technicians. Once the beer is approved, the beer is ready for the packaging line.

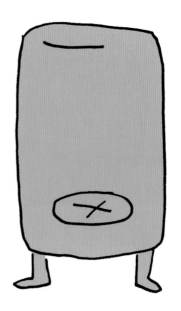

Packaging

Packaging must be done sanitarily in order for the beer to taste its best out in the market. Bottles, cans, and kegs all allow for some space that is filled with CO_2 to keep oxygen out. Oxygen leads to faster degradation of beer.

Cheers to the packaging team!

Bottles are capped or corked, while cans have their tops seamed on.

Packaging can range from a one-person job to operations that fit in a warehouse!

Timeline of Vessels

Earthenware

From the beginning of brewing, earthenware—as simple as a clay pot to fancy, hand-painted porcelain—was essential for thousands of years for fermentation, storage, and drinking.

Wooden barrels

Oak barrels were developed by the Celts around 350 B.C. and are still used today for fermentation.

Aluminum kegs

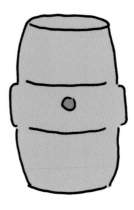

The first airtight metal reusable kegs were aluminum and shaped similar to oak barrels.

Kegs today

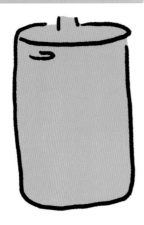

The stainless steel keg with the tapping implement at the top became the worldwide standard for beer dispense in the latter half of the 20th century. Kegs now come in various sizes, the most popular in the U.S. being 5.2 gallons (1/6 barrel) and 15.5 gallons (1/2 barrel).

What is a cask?

In parts of the United Kingdom, beer is packaged while still fermenting into stainless steel casks and then shipped to the pub.

In the cellar of the pub, the publican watches over the casks and knows when they are ready to be served to thirsty patrons.

The beer is pulled up from the cellar by hand pumps. "Real ale" is served slightly warmer and less carbonated than kegged beer.

Bottles!

Bottles come in all different shapes and sizes.

Glass bottles started being used in the 1600s but didn't gain wide popularity till the 19th century.

It's true! Smells just like me.

Green glass doesn't protect against light, which creates a skunky aroma in beers.

Brown glass is best for beer. Using brown glass blocks 98% of light, protecting your beer.

Nice try, Light!

Cans!

Cans are made of aluminum and have been around since the early 1900s.

Cans allow for no light to pass through, making them ideal vessels for beer.

Nice try, Light!

Recyclable, lightweight, and lined with a food-safe liner—cans are great for the outdoors.

From small to large, cans come in all shapes and sizes!

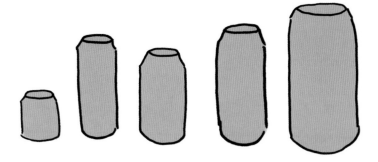

Growlers are filled either from the tap or a special growler filling machine. Growlers are either glass or metal and come in a variety of sizes.

Crowlers are 32 oz. cans filled off the tap at the brewery. They are sealed using a special seamer machine.

They are easy to transport, lightweight, and relatively new to the beer scene.

Foam and Carbonation

Foam is so important! Think of foam as an accessory to beer's job, like a helmet.

Nice hat!

Gorgeous!

Foam concentrates the wonderful smell of beer. This is important to many beer styles.

Carbonation isn't just seeing the bubbles in beer—it's also a mouthfeel sensation! Bubbles range from barely felt to feeling like they are dancing on your tongue.

Different beers have different carbonation levels

Cask Beer
Low

IPAs
Medium

Belgian Trappist

High

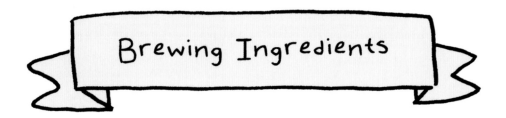

Brewing Ingredients

Barley Malt

Barley is a cereal crop grown across a wide swath of the globe!

There are two types of barley: two-row and six-row.

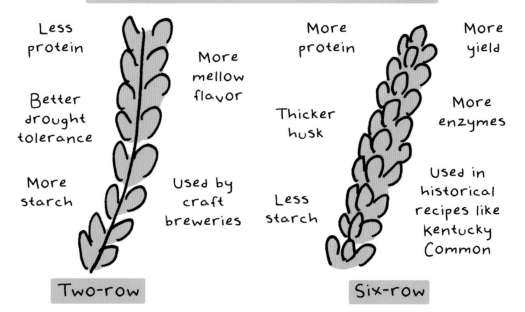

Two-row
- Less protein
- Better drought tolerance
- More starch
- More mellow flavor
- Used by craft breweries

Six-row
- More protein
- Thicker husk
- Less starch
- More yield
- More enzymes
- Used in historical recipes like Kentucky Common

Barley varieties of note

A variety from the U.K. that thrives in maritime climates

Maris Otter

A very important variety from Canada

AC Metcafe

A native barley from Germany

Steffi

Visiting the Malthouse

The malting house is where barley goes from a simple barley kernel to a fully realized malt kernel, ready to be used for beer!

The kernel is harvested in the mid- to late summer and brought to the maltster to start the process.

Steeping

Grains are steeped in 50–60°F water and drained and steeped again over a two day period.

This raises the moisture content so the barley swells and gets large.

Love a good soak

The barley begins to grow!

Over four days under constant air flow and with periodic turning, the barley starts to germinate. This germination process creates starch needed for sugar conversion.

I'm growing!

Kilning

When the barley is dried there is a dramatic change in moisture content, from 40% to 4% moisture by weight.

I'm a whole new kernel.

The time and temperature can vary depending on the type of malt being made.

More heat plus more time equals darker malt.

The finished malt is now allowed to rest before being packaged and sent to your favorite brewery!

Other malting techniques

Stewing: not drying the malt before kilning or roasting it. This is how caramel malts are made as stewing crystallizes the sugar inside.

relaxing

Roasting: using high-temperature, indirect-heat roasting drums to create brown and black malts for dark beers like porters.

How Malt Works

Malt contributes more than just color, flavor, and aroma.

Yeah, so much more!

Once malt is cracked open, the starch is exposed.

At certain temperature rests, starches are converted into sugars with the help of enzymes.

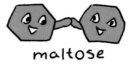

maltose

glucose

It's like opening a lock with a key!

maltotriose

The husk also acts as a filter bed.

When used to make beer, malt gets a good soak to extract the sugar that will later feed the yeast.

Base Malt

Base malts have enough sugars and other nutrients yeast need to be used in 100% of a beer recipe. They are usually lighter in color and make up the bulk malt for most styles.

Base Malts of Note

 Pilsner — The lightest malt and the base of many beer styles, particularly in many European-style beers.

 Pale or Lager — Used in American brewing and imparts a slightly more malty flavor than Pilsner.

 Vienna — Nice toasty notes—100% of Vienna malt can be used to make beers like Vienna lagers.

 Munich — Munich malt is a touch darker than Vienna. Great for Märzens!

Specialty Malt

Specialty malts add color and deeper flavors like chocolate/toffee to beer. They don't have enough sugars to be used on their own.

Specialty Malts of Note

 Biscuit — Kilned at high temperatures for a tasty "bread crust" note.

 Special B — Belgian caramel malt that is stewed then roasted. Great in dark beers!

 Crystal/ Caramel — Malt that is stewed by either kiln or roaster to crystallize sugars. Can be a range of colors.

 Chocolate — Roasted malt that imparts chocolate/coffee flavors and colors to dark beers.

 Black Patent — Very dark, almost burnt malt that adds black color to beer styles like stouts.

Can you brew with grains besides barley?

Yes! We wouldn't have many styles without grains like wheat and oat—they are valuable to many important beer styles, such as German wheat beers, New England IPAs, and oatmeal stouts.

Grains of Note

 **Wheat** — High in protein—can be used raw or malted in many beer styles.

 **Oats** — Adds a silky mouthfeel—can be malted or flaked. Used in stouts and NEIPAs.

 **Sorghum** — Sorghum is an important ingredient in African brewing and gluten-free beers. Used in malted or syrup form.

 **Rye** — High-protein grain that adds a lovely spicy note to many beer styles.

Grains are more than just malt!

The ways we process grains, from heating to rolling and more, can affect their flavor, usage, and dynamic! We couldn't have many important beer styles without these grains.

Processed Grains of Note

 Raw

Unmalted, usually wheat. Raw wheat is used in Belgian styles like witbier and lambic.

 Flaked

Unmalted grains steamed and heated by a roller. Usually oats or corn (maize). Lightens flavor and color of beer.

 Torrified

Similar to creating puffed rice cereal, heat makes moisture in the kernel expand quickly.

 Debittered

Roasting huskless barley to create less astringency (dry/tannic flavors).

Corn (Maize) and Rice

Corn and rice are essential brewing ingredients for many styles, including American Pilsners, Kentucky Common, cream ales, and many others, and is used all over the world.

How corn is used in brewing

Corn can be used either flaked or as grits and offers a cost-effective 100% fermentable source of sugar. Corn was a popular adjunct in American breweries in the 19th century.

How rice is used in brewing

Rice can be used as a fermentable sugar in malted, syrup, or raw form. Popular addition as an adjunct for lagers in tandem with barley. More expensive than corn to use.

Gluten-free Beer

Many people can't drink beer for health or allergy reasons.

So sad!

I'm allergic to gluten!

But beers can be made with grains that have less or no gluten.

Some grains include:

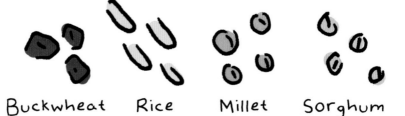

Buckwheat   Rice   Millet   Sorghum

Many styles can be replicated gluten free so no need to worry about issues.

Here's your gluten-free saison!

Non-alcoholic Beer

The world of non-alcoholic beer is becoming more and more vast with lots of different styles.

Some ways NA beer is made

Membrane

ethanol

Letting beer fully ferment and then removing alcohol using dialysis or reverse osmosis.

Heat

Boiling beer in a special vacuum chamber to remove ethanol. Popular in Europe.

Arrested Fermentation

When the brewer stops the fermentation before more ethanol is created by yeast.

It's so great to see more NA beers and many different styles on the shelves!

Water, Water, Everywhere

Water is a VERY important part of brewing.

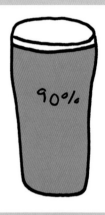

90%

After all, beer is 90% water!

Water can be hard or soft and that can have a profound effect on brewing. Are you brewing with tap water? A stream? Rain?

Water also contributes ions needed for the brewing process.

Important for the health of yeast!

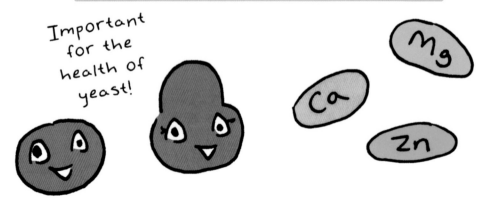

What is Hard Water?

Water can contain a lot of minerals. We call this water "hard."

Water helps with mouthfeel and flavor. Calcium sulfate makes English bitters crisp and refreshing...

...or it can hinder certain beer styles. Calcium sulfate in dark beers can make the beer very bitter and harsh.

Brewers manipulate water using filters or adding minerals to brew good beer.

Famous Brewing Cities and their Water Chemistry

Cities traditionally created styles based on what they had available—that included water sources.

Plzeň, Czech Republic

Very soft water with almost no minerals. Perfect for golden lagers.

Burton-on-Trent, England

High sulfate levels make hoppy beers crisp and dry. Perfect for bitters!

Munich, Germany

Calcium carbonate adds sweetness and body to dark lagers.

Dortmund, Germany

Mineral-rich water that adds a rocky minerality to its signature export lager.

Dublin, Ireland

Calcium carbonate adds more fullness and sweetness to its stouts.

All Hail the Hop!

Hops are important in many ways! For one, they give flavor and aroma to beer.

They also have preservative properties to help keep beer fresher longer and aid in head retention.

Hops are SUPER for beer!

Hop Anatomy

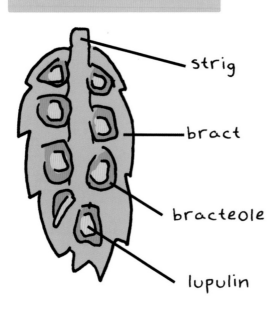

— strig

— bract

— bracteole

— lupulin

Let's go see where hops are grown.

To Yakima

Visiting the Hop Field

Hop fields can vary in size. Some are very large!

Hops are grown on very tall trellises, which in Germany are taller than in the U.S.

Lines are strung and hops are planted in the spring each year.

Hop cones grows on a "bine."

A bine is a stem that grows around a central location like a rope!

English hop workers used stilts to string lines back in the day.

Now done by machines, hop picking was once a family affair, with thousands of pickers coming from the city to make extra money and enjoy the country air.

Hop harvesting is done in August/September in the Northern Hemisphere.

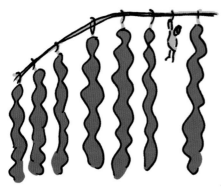

Harvested hop bines are attached to hooks in the processing facility and go for a ride to a special rake that removes the cones.

Cones are raked off and put on a conveyer and then the hops are kilned. They are layered 2-3 ft. deep.

Smells so good!

Hops are dried with gas-fired kilns for 8-10 hours to get their moisture down. They are then left to cool in piles before being baled.

How Hops Work

Once the wort is boiling, it's the hops turn to shine.

Come on in, it's HOT!

Hops are added to boiling wort so that "isomerization" can occur.

Isomerization—hops contain alpha acids, which change (isomerize) at high temperatures. These new "iso-alpha acids" are what impart bitterness.

This is important for very bitter beers like Double IPAs.

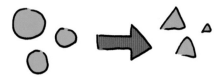

Some hop varieties have low alpha acid levels and some have a LOT!

Low: Saaz

Low/Med: Aramis

Med/High: Target

High: Zeus

Hops can be used in all sorts of ways!

Whole Cone
This is the dried version of the whole hop flower. Most traditional but now passed over in favor of hop pellets.

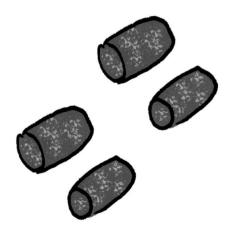

Hop Pellets
Hop pellets are more concentrated and save lots of space for brewers. This is the most popular way hops are used nowadays.

Advanced Hop Products
Hops can be made into extracts that remove vegetative product altogether and are shelf stable.

How Are Hops Categorized?

Bittering Hops
Hops prized for their bittering features and are used mainly at the beginning of the boil.

Zeus

Galena

Herkules

Magnum

Amarillo

Hallertau

East Kent Golding

Riwaka

Aroma Hops
Hops prized for aromas (these can vary widely from pine to melon to flowers!). These are used at the end of the boil.

Dual-Purpose Hops
Hops that can be used for both bittering early in the boil or later for aroma/flavor.

Cascade

Galaxy

Target

Simcoe

American Hops

Flavor attributes include:

citrus   pine   melon   dank

American hops are mostly grown in the Pacific Northwest.

Washington   Oregon   Idaho

Here are some of my favorites:

Citra   Mosaic

Centennial   Strata   Amarillo   Chinook

What Are Noble Hops?

Noble hops are the four German/Czech hops used in most classic German and Czech beers.

Noble hops come across as spicy, floral, and earthy. The perfect complement to those German and Czech lagers!

Na zdraví!   Prost!

These hop varieties have a special flavor that just screams "noble."

Saaz

Spalt Spalter

Hallertau Mittelfrüh

Tettnang

German Hops

Flavor attributes include:

herbal

hay

spice

floral

German hops are grown in southern Germany in the Lake Constance, Hallertau, and Elbe-Saale regions.

Lake Constance

Some popular varieties:

Perle

Hersbrucker

Magnum

Saphir

British Hops

Flavor attributes include:

herbal   lavender   marmalade   floral

British hops are grown in Kent in the South East and in Herefordshire and Worcestershire in the West Midlands.

Kent Countryside

Some popular varieties:

Target   East Kent Golding   Fuggle   Pilgrim

European Hops

Flavor attributes include:

floral   hay   earthy   herbal

Besides Germany, special hop varieties come from France, Slovenia, Czech Republic, and Poland.

Alsace, France

Some popular varieties:

   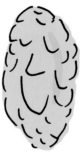

Styrian
Golding   Lublin   Strisselspalt   Sladek

Southern Hemisphere Hops

Flavor attributes include:

tropical   white wine   mango   passion fruit

Southern Hemisphere hops are grown in New Zealand, South Africa, and Australia.

Tasmania

Some popular varieties:

Galaxy   Vic Secret   Motueka   Nelson Sauvin

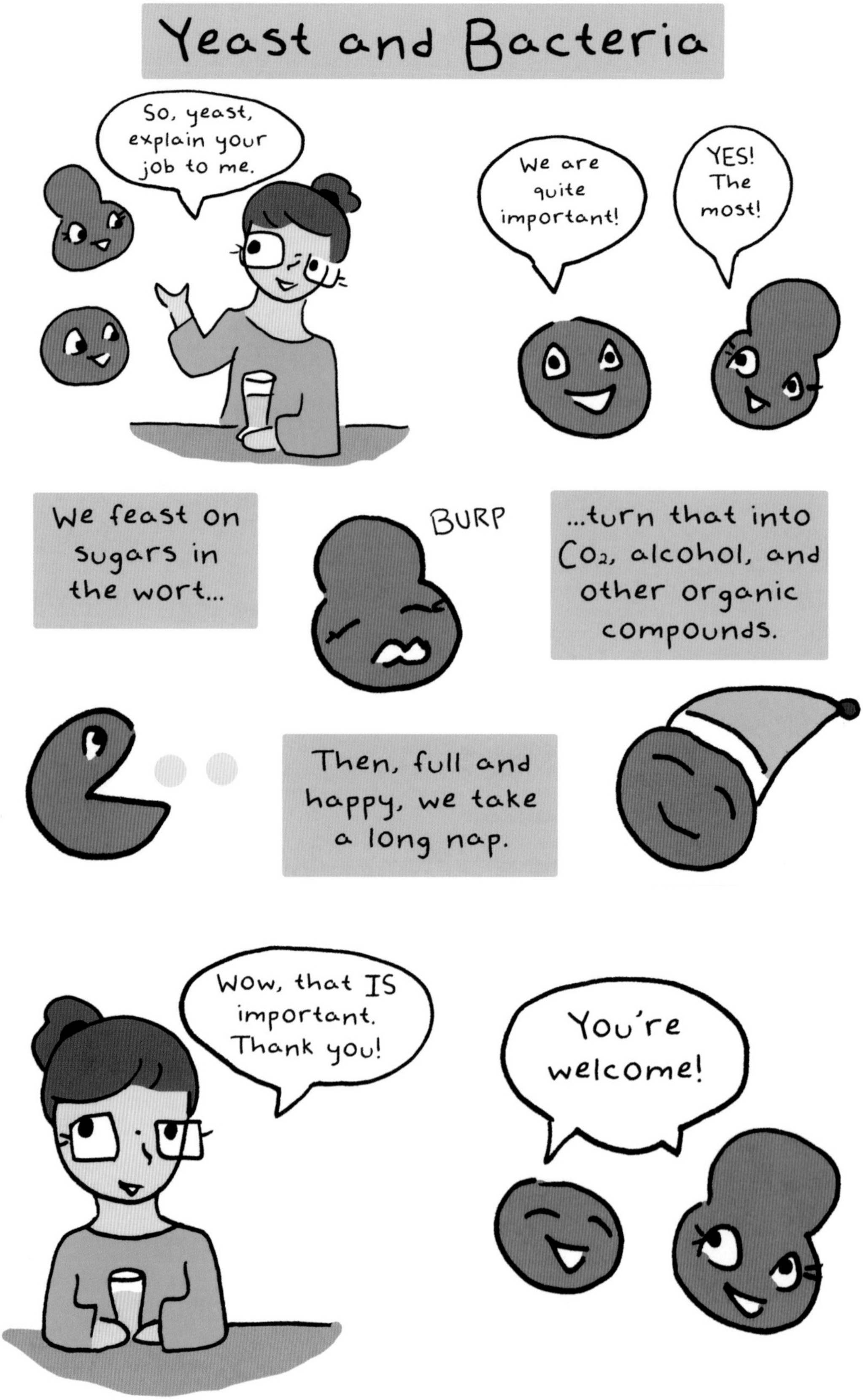
Yeast and Bacteria
So, yeast, explain your job to me.
We are quite important!
YES! The most!
We feast on sugars in the wort...
BURP
...turn that into CO_2, alcohol, and other organic compounds.
Then, full and happy, we take a long nap.
Wow, that IS important. Thank you!
You're welcome!

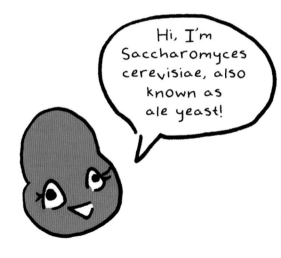

Hi, I'm Saccharomyces cerevisiae, also known as ale yeast!

I ferment at temperatures from 60-95°F. I finish the job in about one week.

I'm "top fermenting," meaning I rise quickly to the top of the fermentor. Great for open fermentation styles.

Ale yeast encompasses many styles!

Bitters!   Belgians!   Stouts!   IPAs!

Different ale yeast strains create different byproducts, some that are characteristic of certain styles.

Weizen yeast!

Banana

Clove

Saison yeast!

Pepper

Clove

English yeast!

Pear

Apple

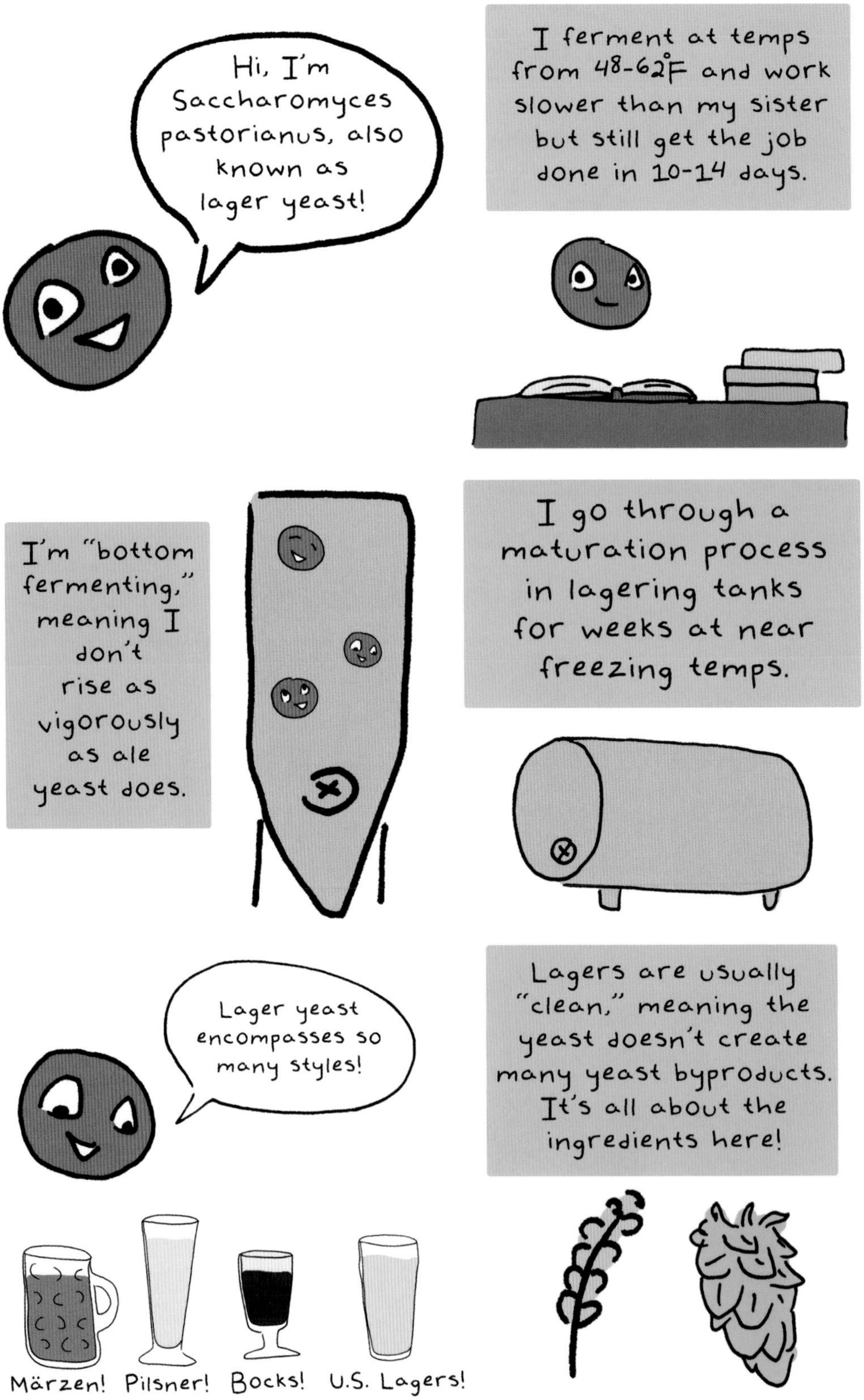
Hi, I'm Saccharomyces pastorianus, also known as lager yeast!
I ferment at temps from 48-62°F and work slower than my sister but still get the job done in 10-14 days.
I'm "bottom fermenting," meaning I don't rise as vigorously as ale yeast does.
I go through a maturation process in lagering tanks for weeks at near freezing temps.
Lager yeast encompasses so many styles!
Märzen!
Pilsner!
Bocks!
U.S. Lagers!
Lagers are usually "clean," meaning the yeast doesn't create many yeast byproducts. It's all about the ingredients here!

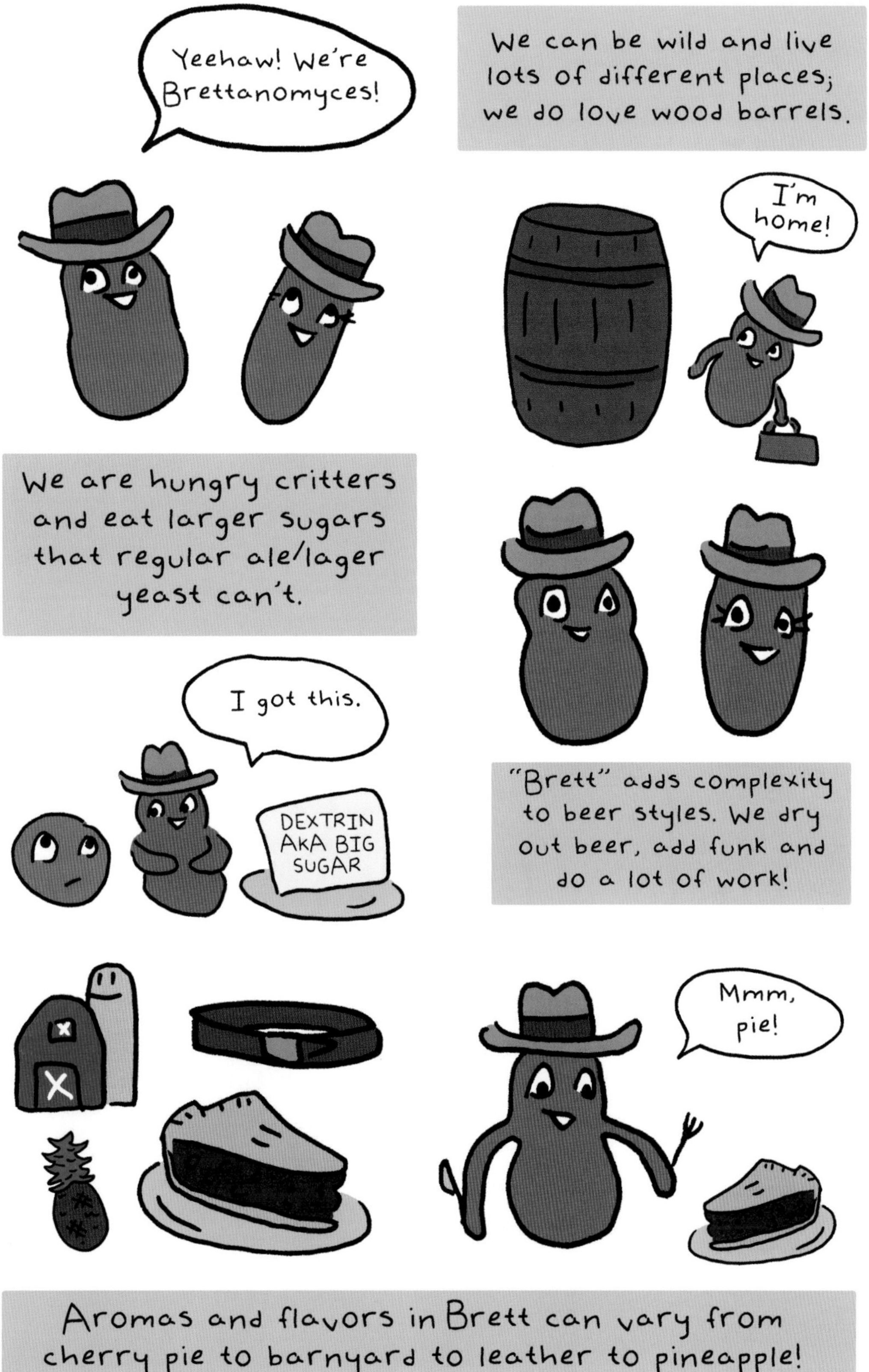
Yeehaw! We're Brettanomyces!
We can be wild and live lots of different places; we do love wood barrels.
I'm home!
We are hungry critters and eat larger sugars that regular ale/lager yeast can't.
I got this.
DEXTRIN AKA BIG SUGAR
"Brett" adds complexity to beer styles. We dry out beer, add funk and do a lot of work!
Mmm, pie!
Aromas and flavors in Brett can vary from cherry pie to barnyard to leather to pineapple!

Hey, I'm Pediococcus bacteria.

And I'm Lactobacillus bacteria. It's super great to meet you.

We can be a vital part of all your favorite beer recipes. If you love sour beers, we in part did that! We create lactic acid that creates that tart flavor.

Gose

Berliner Weisse

Lambic

Oud Bruin

Sometimes we're bad and get where we shouldn't be, like dirty draft lines.

Cozy!

We bacteria are super beer geeks. We love beer almost as much as you!

Cheers, mate!

Cheers, friend!

I'm Acetobacter!

When I get around oxygen, I create acetic acid. Acetic acid makes vinegar.

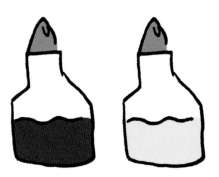

I can do this in all beers, but sometimes I unintentionally get carried away and a little rowdy. For that, I am sorry.

My proudest work is Flanders Red Ale. Lovely!

Yikes!

For styles where I'm not supposed to be, keep oxygen levels low!

What is Mixed Fermentation?

Definition: using both beer yeast and bacteria or Brettanomyces to brew a beer that is tart or funky.

Hey friend!

Hello pal!

A brewer will brew a "base" beer style.

Then it can go into a barrel where bacteria already live...

...Or both yeast and bacteria can be added by the brewer.

Sometimes fruit is added as well for natural acidity.

They can take a long time to develop but they are worth the wait!

What is Barrel Aging?

Back in the day (and sometimes still today), a brewery would age all its beer in barrels; sometimes on the oak, sometimes in pitch-lined barrels to prevent flavor transfer from the wood.

Barrels are now used for specialty beers. Barrels today are mainly made of oak, usually French or American.

Second-use spirits/liquor barrels are popular now.

whiskey

bourbon

wine

Barrels can also be home to wild bacteria and yeast!

Barrels can also be made larger than the standard barrel.

Puncheon is 84-144 U.S. gallons in size.

Foeder is any oak vessel larger than 160 U.S. gallons.

Off-Flavors in Beer

Oh no! This beer has an off-flavor. How sad.

Off-flavors can be created by ingredients...

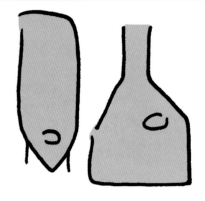

...by process...

...or by time itself.

Sometimes beer can just go bad.

Let's learn why.

Dimethyl Sulfide (DMS)

creamed corn

cabbage

tomato juice in dark beers

Where does it come from?

Malt derived! A naturally occurring creation of malt that is usually boiled off through steam vapor during the boil.

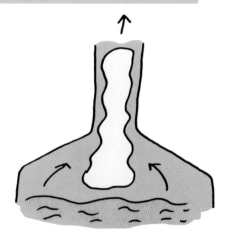

Protective actions

*Boil your wort for at least 60 minutes.

*Make sure you are using high-quality malts.

Low amounts allowed in:

Pale Lagers

Acetaldehyde

green apple   latex paint   pumpkin

Where does it come from?

Pulling the yeast too early before it has time to clean up all its byproducts; a sign a beer is "green."

Protective actions

*Let beer finish fermenting.

*Ensure healthy fermentation conditions.

Low amounts allowed in:

American Light Lagers

Diacetyl

butter

movie theatre popcorn

butterscotch

Where does it come from?

It's a precursor molecule that leaches out of yeast cells during their snacking phase. Healthy yeast should clean up the diacetyl and turn it into a flavorless compound but sometimes they're too tired. Also can be a part of dirty draft line infection.

Protective actions

*Use healthy yeast and give them enough time to clean up all diacetyl.

*Clean draft lines every two weeks.

Low amounts allowed in:

Bohemian Pilsner

Oxidation

wet newspaper

sherry

cardboard

Where does it come from?

When beer ages or is exposed to oxygen, malt and hop compounds break down. Oxygen and beer are NOT friends.

Protective actions

*Keep beer cold as that slows oxidation.

*Drink beer fresh unless the style dictates.

Low amounts allowed in:

Strong ales where aging adds complexity

Lactic and Acetic Acid

spoiled milk

vinegar

lemon

Where do they come from?

From bacteria—when beer isn't meant to be sour but is, that means there's an infection in the beer. Could be from dirty draft lines! Yuck! Lactic acid is softer and also has no aroma while acetic acid is sharper and has an odor.

EW!

Protective actions

*Make sure oxygen stays out of beer.

*Good brewery and draft line hygiene.

Low amounts allowed in:

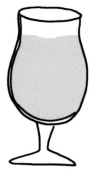

Sour beer styles

Hydrogen Sulfide (H2S)

rotten eggs

sewer

volcano/
sulfur springs

Where does it come from?

A byproduct from yeast, particularly lager yeast. Also from water high in sulfate. Only an aroma in most cases.

Protective actions

*Treat brewing water.

*Allow yeast to finish fermenting.

Low amounts allowed in:

British Bitters and Lagers

Esters

red apple

pear

banana

Where do they come from?

A byproduct from yeast, esters are in all beers but noticeable in ales. In low amounts, there's a lovely fruitiness. Too much can be solventy.

Protective actions

Beers fermented colder will have less esters.

Can be pleasant in:

Ales

Phenols

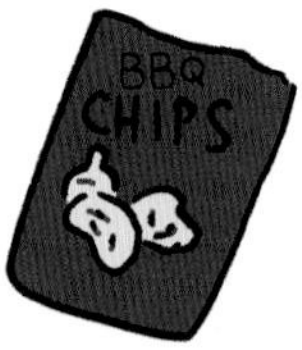
BBQ
CHIPS

BBQ chips

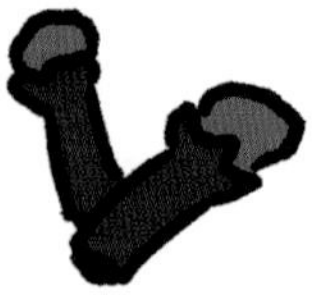

clove

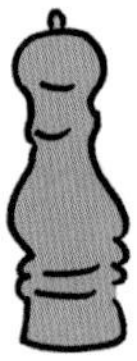

white pepper

Where do they come from?

A byproduct from yeast and an important flavor compound for German wheat ales like hefeweizen and Belgian styles like tripels and saisons.

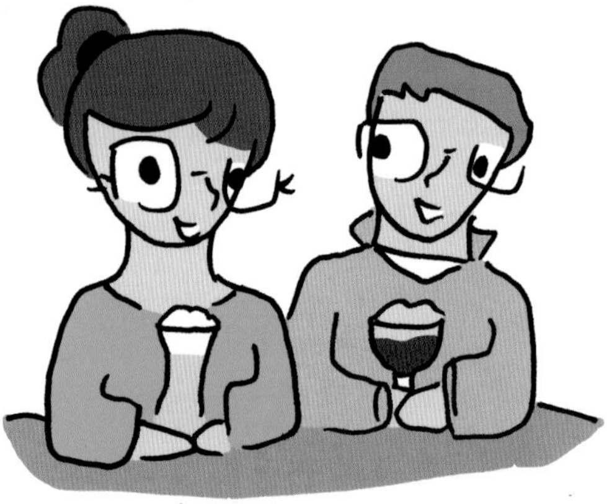

Protective actions

*Watch fermentation temperatures.

*Practice good brewing hygiene.

*If brewing a beer style that has phenols - choose a yeast strain that can create phenols.

Can be pleasant in:

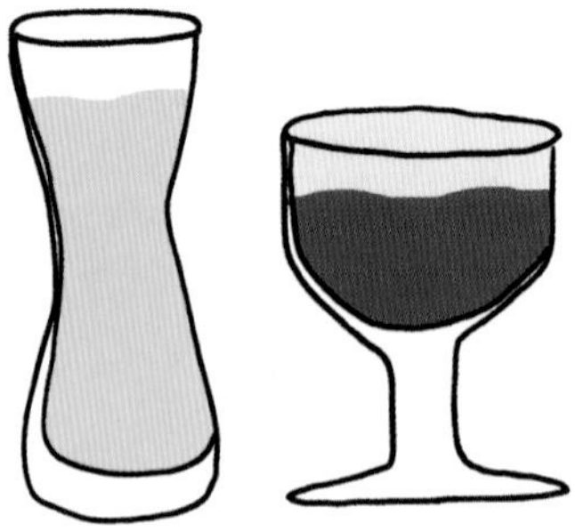

German weissbiers
Belgian styles

Autolysis

rubber

soy sauce

meaty

Where does it come from?

Yeast cells get old or stressed out. When that happens, they can self-destruct and the organic compounds they release can flavor the beer.

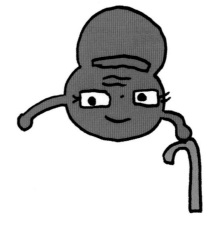

Protective actions

*Drink beer fresh!

*Make sure the yeast is happy.

*Pull finished beer off of yeast as soon as fermentation is complete.

Low amounts allowed in:

NO!

Isovaleric Acid

parmesan
cheese

sweaty
socks

body
odor

Where does it come from?

When hop
material gets
old or hops
aren't kept cold
they can start
to break down,
like other
vegetables do.

Oh boy,
it's hot!

Protective actions

*Use fresh hops.

*Keep hops
refrigerated/cold.

Low amounts
allowed in:

NO!

Lightstruck

skunk

rubber

fresh coffee

Where does it come from?

When hop acids react with light, a skunky compound is created. Usually associated with green or clear beer bottles but can happen if beer sits in the sun for just a few minutes.

Cheers to sunshine!

Protective actions

*Cans and brown bottles protect against this.

*Keep beer out of direct light.

Low amounts allowed in:

NO!

Beer and Food

My favorite part of the day; time to eat!

Hmmm, I'm drinking a Pilsner. What would I pair with that?

Lucky for beer drinkers, beer and food are excellent friends. Together, they help us have our best meals possible.

Knowing simple pairing guidelines can elevate beer to a whole new level.

Beer and food—it's magic!

No offense to wine, but beer's myriad flavors and intensities work wonders with food.

Use the four c's to master beer and food pairings!

Cut

Contrast

Complement

Clash

We'll use this salad to help us.

Check out the next page!

The Four Cs: Mixed Green Salad with Citrus Dressing

Complement

When a beer is complementary to the food.

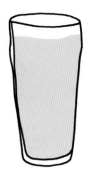

A blonde ale will complement the herbal greens and citrus dressing.

Contrast

When a flavor from the beer heightens another flavor.

A salty Gose will contrast the fruity, sweet dressing.

Cut

When the beer cuts an element of the food. I call it the "mouth napkin."

The high carbonation of a witbier will cleanse your palate.

Clash

When the beer and food flavors fight each other making for a mess.

The high ABV of an English barleywine will overwhelm the salad.

Pairing Advice

Beer acts as fruit, bread, and other great side dishes to food.

Let the beer be the side dish!

Vienna lager becomes a bready complement to spaghetti.

Hefeweizen adds more fruit to pancakes.

A fruit lambic adds more tartness to a cheesecake.

Match intensties!

Sushi with blonde ale or American stout?

Blonde ale! An American stout would blow out all the flavors of the delicate sushi. Pairing lighter food with lighter beers is always a good bet.

Favorite Pairings!

Breakfast

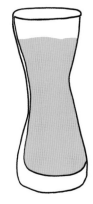

Eggs Benedict and a hefeweizen: Forget mimosas—this high-carbonation fruity beer will be an excellent companion.

Lunch

Tacos and New England IPA: Citrus haze meets salty/spicy for a tasty symphony of flavor.

Dinner

Steak and tripel: The high carbonation and alcohol cleanses your palate; great contrast of salty/sweet.

Dessert

Brownies and imperial stout: So many complementary chocolate flavors!

Beer and Cheese!

Follow the same rules as before and enjoy the experience of beer and cheese!

Brie & saison

Alpine cheese & U.S. brown ale

Cheddar & English IPA

Stilton & barleywine

Blue cheese & double IPA

Helles & Colby Jack

Manchego & robust porter

Mozzarella & hefeweizen

Aged Gouda & wee heavy

The World of
Beer Styles

What is a Beer Style?

There are many different beer styles throughout the world. But how are they categorized?

Think about dogs—some dogs are very small and some are large; they are all different colors. Some are fierce and some are tame.

Beers are the same way. They can be dark or light, higher or lower in alcohol, and can encompass all manner of flavors.

Something for all!

Alcohol Level Key
Low: Under 5%
Medium: 5-7.5%
High: 7.5% & up

In this next section we'll talk about the many popular beer styles. Not all beer styles made the book so consult the Brewers Association guidelines for a complete list!

Belgium and France

Belgium's beer scene is truly wonderful. They take brewing very seriously. From unique brewing regimens to specialty glassware to protected styles—Belgians love their beer fiercely!

The Belgian brewing tradition is hundreds of years old. Beer styles like lambics, saisons, and dubbels have been part of life here for centuries.

Pull up a chair at a cafe, order a bottle, and let's learn all about the world of Belgian beers!

Trappist Single

Trappist singles are low-alcohol beers usually made only for the monks to have with meals.
A great session beer.

Aroma/Flavor

Clove   Lemon

Pear   Floral

Food Pairings:
Mussels
Salad

Ingredients

 Continental hops

Pale malt

 Belgian ale yeast

Alcohol Content:
Low
Color:
Yellow to Golden
Bitterness:
Low/Medium

Belgian Pale Ale

Belgian pale ales are popular in the city of Antwerp. They are excellent with all manner of cuisines.

Food Pairings:
Grilled cheese
Fish and chips

Alcohol Content:
Low/Medium
Color:
Golden to Amber
Bitterness:
Low/Medium

Aroma/Flavor

Pear

Toast

Honey

Orange

Ingredients

 Continental hops

Pale and
Munich malts

 Ale yeast

Belgian Blonde Ale

Belgian blonde ales became a style due to the popularity of Pilsners (although the only thing they have in common with a Pilsner is the color). A great food beer or perfect to enjoy in an iconic Belgian cafe.

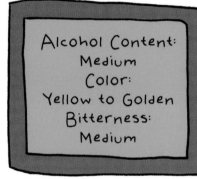

Food Pairings:
Fries
Mussels

Aroma/Flavor

Clove   Earthy

Perfume   Honey

Ingredients

 Continental hops

 Pilsner malt plus sugar

 Belgian ale yeast

Alcohol Content:
Medium
Color:
Yellow to Golden
Bitterness:
Medium

Belgian Strong Blonde Ale

Belgian strong blonde ales are excellent with a wide variety of foods. I highly recommend them with Thanksgiving dinner!

Aroma/Flavor

Orange

Honey

Pear

White pepper

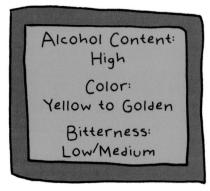

Food Pairings:
Turkey
Fruit tart

Ingredients

 Continental hops

Pilsner malt plus sugar

  Belgian ale yeast

Alcohol Content:
High

Color:
Yellow to Golden

Bitterness:
Low/Medium

Belgian Dubbel

Dubbels have monastic roots but were modernized in the 20th century.

Food Pairings:
Pork loin
Blue cheese

Alcohol Content:
Medium
Color:
Amber to Brown
Bitterness:
Low

Aroma/Flavor

Caramel

Clove

Banana

Plum

Ingredients

Continental hops

Pilsner, Munich, dark, and wheat malts plus sugar

Belgian ale yeast

Belgian Tripel

Tripel is a Trappist style invented by Westmalle Brewery in Belgium.

Food Pairings
Steak frites
Roast turkey

Aroma/Flavor

Pear   Honey

Pepper   Clove

Ingredients

Alcohol Content:
High
Color:
Yellow to Golden
Bitterness:
Medium

 Continental hops

 Pilsner malt,
perhaps some sugar

 Belgian ale yeast

Belgian Quadrupel

"Quads" are the strongest of the Trappist ales.

Aroma/Flavor

 Caramel

 Rose

 Raisin

 Clove

Food Pairing:
Venison
Caramel custard

Ingredients

 Continental hops

 Pilsner, Munich, dark malt, and sugar

Belgian ale yeast

Alcohol Content:
High
Color:
Amber to Brown
Bitterness:
Medium

111

Belgian Witbier

Modern witbier originates from Belgium in the town of Hoegaarden, where it is still made to this day.

Aroma/Flavor

 Bread dough

Cracker

Orange

Coriander

Food Pairing:
Mussels
Salad

Ingredients

 Continental hops

 Pilsner malt, raw wheat and flaked oats, plus spices

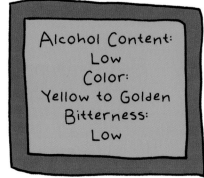

Alcohol Content:
Low
Color:
Yellow to Golden
Bitterness:
Low

 Witbier ale yeast

Oud Bruin

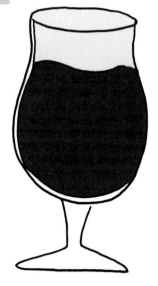

Oud bruin originated in East Flanders and is a tart brown ale that's been made for hundreds of years. It is aged for months in fermentors, which are usually stainless steel rather than oak.

Aroma/Flavor

Chocolate

Orange

Sherry

Raisin

Food Pairings:
Steak
Lobster

Ingredients

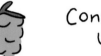
Continental or U.K. hops

Pilsner, Munich, wheat, black patent, aromatic, and Special B

Ale yeast plus Lactobacillus

Alcohol Content: Low/Medium
Color: Deep Amber to Dark Brown
Bitterness: Low

Flanders Red Ale

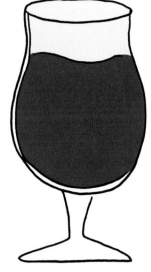

Flanders red ales come from the Flemish speaking part of Belgium. Historically aged in large oak foeders and then blended. Tart and tasty!

Aroma/Flavor

 Cherry

 Vanilla

 Ketchup

 Orange

Food Pairings:
Pork loin
Prime rib

Ingredients

 Continental or U.K. hops

 Pale, Vienna, Munich, wheat, and Special B malts plus maybe flaked corn

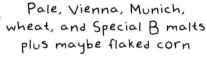 Ale yeast plus Pediococcus, Brettanomyces, Lactobacillus

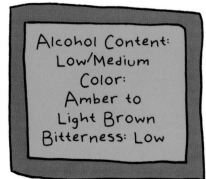

Alcohol Content:
Low/Medium
Color:
Amber to
Light Brown
Bitterness: Low

Belgian Lambic

Lambics are spontaneously fermented still or semi-sparkling beers made in the Senne River Valley in Belgium.

Food Pairings:
Goat cheese
Salad

Alcohol Content:
Low/Medium
Color:
Yellow to Golden
Bitterness:
Low

Aroma/Flavor

Hay

Floral

Tart apple

Lemon

Ingredients

Aged hops

Pilsner malt and raw wheat

Spontaneous fermentation

Gueuze

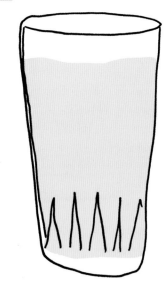

A gueuze (pronounced GOOZ) is a blend of different aged lambics, usually one, two, and three years in age.

Food Pairings:
Oysters
Mussels

Aroma/Flavor

Hay

Leather

Tart apple

Oak

Ingredients

Aged hops

Pilsner malt and raw wheat

Spontaneous fermentation

Alcohol Content:
Low/Medium
Color:
Golden
Bitterness:
Low

Fruit Lambic

Fruit lambics use a variety of fruits—cherry (kriek) and raspberry (framboise) are most popular.

Aroma/Flavor

Fruit used   Hay

Barnyard   Leather

Food Pairings:
Cheesecake
Brownies

Ingredients

 Aged hops

 Pilsner malt and raw wheat

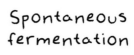 Spontaneous fermentation

Alcohol Content:
Low/Medium
Color:
Varies
Bitterness:
Low

Saison

Saisons are a broad class of beer style from the Wallonia region of Belgium and eastern France originally made with ingredients found in the farmhouse.

Food Pairings:
Roast chicken
Mushroom tart

Aroma/Flavor

Lemon   Pepper

Herbal   Cracker

Ingredients

Alcohol Content:
Low to High
Color:
Gold to Amber
Bitterness:
Low

Continental hops

Pilsner malt plus maybe oats, spelt

 Saison ale yeast

Bière de Garde

Bière de garde ("beer to keep" in English) is a style from Northern France. It can be blonde, amber, or brown in color and was historically brewed in spring.

Aroma/Flavor

Red apple

Toffee

Herbal

Toast

Food Pairings:
Roast chicken
Mushroom tart

Ingredients

French hops

Pilsner, Vienna, and Munich malts

Ale or
lager yeast

Alcohol Content:
Medium/High
Color:
Gold to Brown
Bitterness:
Low

United Kingdom and Ireland

Beer has been brewed in Ireland and the U.K. for thousands of years!

Since the invention of the popular porter, modern English, Scottish, and Irish beers have been an important part of the brewing landscape.

Pull up a seat at the pub, get a fresh pint of cask bitter or nitrogenated stout, and let's explore the varied styles of these wonderful countries.

Bitter

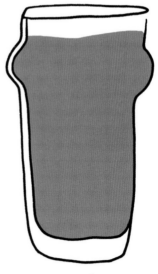

Bitter comes in three strengths: ordinary, best, and strong. Perfect for long days and nights at the pub.

Aroma/Flavor

Marmalade

Toast

Food Pairings:
Scotch egg
Veggie burger

Floral

Earthy

Ingredients

U.K. hops

Pale and crystal malts; maybe sugar, corn or wheat.

English ale yeast

Alcohol Content:
Low/Medium
Color: Deep Gold
to Brown
Bitterness:
Medium/High

Scottish-Style Ales

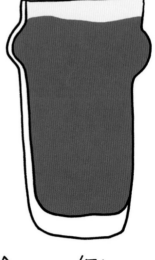

Scottish styles are malt-focused ales. Historically named after the cost of a barrel, Scottish styles still go by 60, 70, or 80 shilling ales with 60 being the lowest ABV.

Aroma/Flavor

 Caramel

 Toffee

 Pear

 Earthy

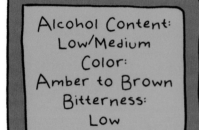

Food Pairings:
Bread puddings
Fish and chips

Ingredients

 U.K. hops

Alcohol Content:
Low/Medium
Color:
Amber to Brown
Bitterness:
Low

 Pale malt and corn; can use a variety of malts or sugar too

 Scottish ale yeast

Wee Heavy or Scotch Ale

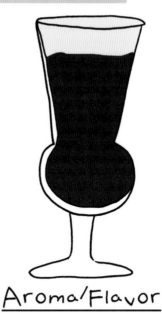

Scotch ale, a rich and warming brew, is served in a thistle glass, designed to look like the national emblem of Scotland.

Aroma/Flavor

Toffee

Raisin

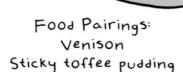

Plum

Caramel

Food Pairings:
Venison
Sticky toffee pudding

Ingredients

U.K. hops

Pale and crystal malts plus roasted barley

Scottish ale yeast

Alcohol Content:
Medium to High
Color:
Amber to Brown
Bitterness:
Medium

English Summer Ale

A sessionable golden ale that's one of the newest English beer styles. Perfect for drinking outside with good friends.

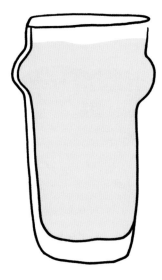

Aroma/Flavor

Earthy

Lavender

Tea

Grapefruit

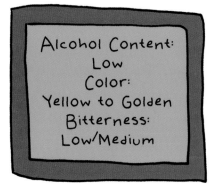

Food Pairings:
Salad
Salmon

Ingredients

U.K. or
U.S. hops

Pale and
wheat malts

English
ale yeast

Alcohol Content:
Low
Color:
Yellow to Golden
Bitterness:
Low/Medium

English IPA

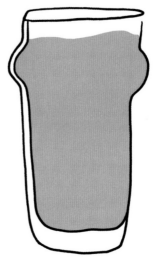

The original IPA shows off the versatility of hops grown in England.

Food Pairings:
Fish and chips
Curry

Alcohol Content:
Low/Medium
Color:
Golden to Amber
Bitterness:
Medium/High

Aroma/Flavor

Herbal

Marmalade

Tea

Floral

Ingredients

U.K. hops

Pale and
crystal malts

English
ale yeast

British Strong Ale

British strong ales are also known as "winter warmers;" most excellent for colder weather.

Aroma/Flavor

Graham cracker

Toffee

Pear

Plum

Food Pairings:
Gingerbread
Prime rib

Ingredients

U.K. hops

Pale and crystal malts plus maybe dark malt, corn, flaked barley, or wheat

English ale yeast

Alcohol Content: Medium/High
Color: Deep Gold to Dark Brown
Bitterness: Medium/High

Old Ale

Old ales were historically held for long periods of time and drank as is or used for blending. Aged character is desired.

Food Pairings:
Beef Wellington
Fruit pie

Aroma/Flavor

Port wine   Dark toast

Caramel   Raisin

Alcohol Content: Medium/High
Color: Amber to Dark Brown
Bitterness: Medium/High

Ingredients

U.K. hops

Pale and crystal malts plus maybe dark malt, corn, flaked barley, or wheat

English ale yeast

English-Style Barleywine

English barleywines have been around for centuries and are the strongest British style. Made with lots of malt, a winter sipper perfect for that drafty castle.

Aroma/Flavor

Port wine   Dark toast

Caramel   Raisin

Food Pairings:
Stilton cheese
Sticky toffee pudding

Ingredients

 U.K. hops

 Pale and crystal malts

Alcohol Content: Medium/High
Color: Amber to Dark Brown
Bitterness: Medium/High

English ale yeast

English Porter

English porter was the first beer produced on an industrial scale. Large breweries pumped out millions of barrels to meet demand.

Aroma/Flavor

Dark toast

Caramel

Chocolate

Licorice

Food Pairings:
Pork pie
BBQ chicken

Ingredients

U.K. hops

Pale, crystal, and chocolate malts; historically made with brown malt

English ale yeast

Alcohol Content: Low/Medium
Color: Brown to Dark Brown
Bitterness: Low/Medium

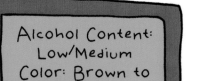

129

English Brown Ale

I'm nuts for it!

English brown ales are made with U.K. ingredients and sometimes have a 'nutty' flavor. There are no nuts used to make this beer.

Aroma/Flavor

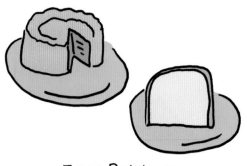

Food Pairings:
Pork pie
Alpine cheese

Nutty

Toffee

Pear

Toast

Ingredients

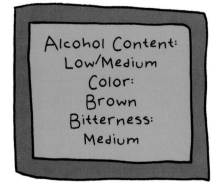

Alcohol Content:
Low/Medium
Color:
Brown
Bitterness:
Medium

U.K. hops

Pale, crystal, and chocolate malts

Ale yeast

Dark Mild

Dark milds were a popular style from the late 19th to mid-20th century in England. In the past, "mild" referred to any beer that was served fresh.

Food Pairings:
Shepherd's pie
Mild cheddar

Alcohol Content:
Low
Color: Brown to
Dark Brown
Bitterness:
Low

Aroma/Flavor

Plum

Toast

Chocolate

Licorice

Ingredients

U.K. hops

Pale, crystal, and chocolate malts

English ale yeast

Milk/Sweet Stout

Milk stouts have a rich, full mouthfeel due to the addition of the unfermentable sugar, lactose.

Food Pairings:
Chocolate cake
Brownies

Alcohol Content:
Low/Medium
Color: Dark Brown
to Black
Bitterness:
Low

Aroma/Flavor

 Chocolate

 Coffee

 Pear

 Vanilla

Ingredients

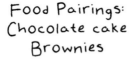 U.K. hops

 Pale, chocolate, and black malts

 English or U.S. ale yeast

Russian Imperial Stout

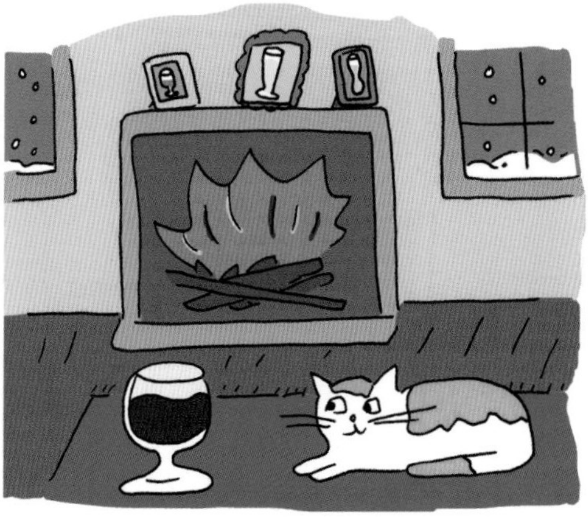

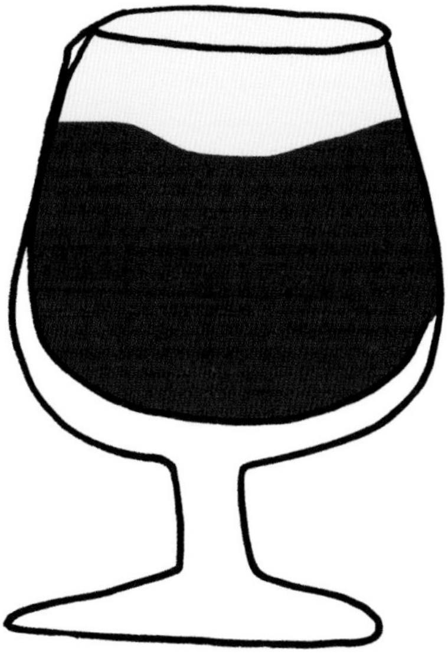

A high-ABV stout popular with Russian royalty in the 18th century and now still as popular as ever! Perfect for snowy evenings.

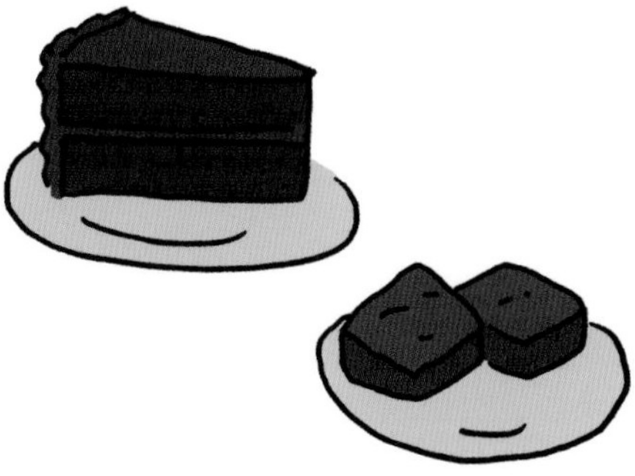

Food Pairings:
Chocolate cake
Brownies

Aroma/Flavor

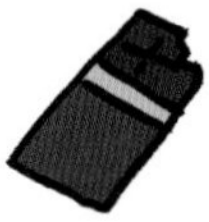

Chocolate

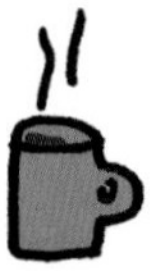

Coffee

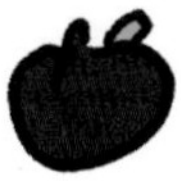

Plum

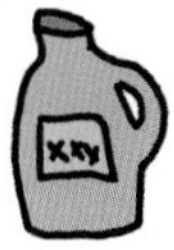
XXX

Alcohol

Alcohol Content: High
Color: Dark Brown to Black
Bitterness: High

Ingredients

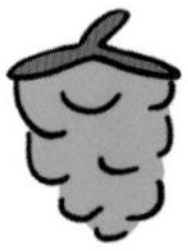

U.K. or U.S. hops

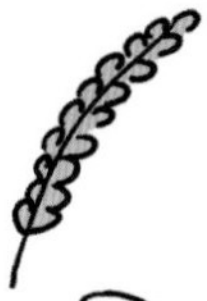

Pale, black, chocolate, and crystal malts

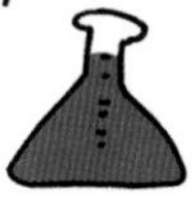

English or U.S. ale yeast

Oatmeal Stout

Oatmeal stouts are made with oats, which gives this styly a silky mouthfeel.

Aroma/Flavor

 Coffee

 Plum

 Chocolate

 Caramel

Food Pairings:
Pancakes
French toast

Alcohol Content:
Low/Medium
Color:
Brown to Black
Bitterness:
Low/Medium

Ingredients

 U.K. hops

Pale, Munich, and chocolate malts plus flaked oats

 English or U.S. ale yeast

Irish Red Ale

Irish red ales are a modern Irish style. This style is similar to a bitter but with less hops and brewed with roasted barley.

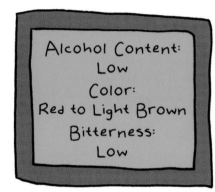

Food Pairings:
Fish and chips
Grilled cheese sandwich

Alcohol Content:
Low
Color:
Red to Light Brown
Bitterness:
Low

Aroma/Flavor

 Cereal

 Toast

 Earthy

 Toffee

Ingredients

 U.K. hops

Pale and crystal malts plus roasted barley

 Irish ale yeast

135

Irish Dry Stout

The Guinness Brewery in Dublin, Ireland is the creator of this style. They also invented the nitro tap that it is now usually served on!

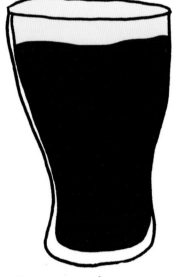

Food Pairings:
Oysters
Beef stew

Alcohol Content:
Low/Medium
Color:
Dark Brown
to Black
Bitterness: Medium

Aroma/Flavor

Chocolate

Caramel

Coffee

Burnt toast

Ingredients

U.K. hops

Pale malt, flaked barley, and roasted barley

Irish ale yeast

Export Stout

Brewed stronger and hoppier for the export market. One of the most popular beer styles in the world, especially in warm climates.

Food Pairings:
Beef stew
Fish and chips

Alcohol Content:
Medium/High
Color:
Dark Brown
to Black
Bitterness: Medium

Aroma/Flavor

 Chocolate

 Coffee

Molasses

Burnt toast

Ingredients

 U.K. hops

 Pale, crystal, and black malts plus roasted barley

 Irish ale yeast

Germany and the Czech Republic

Germany and the Czech Republic are where lagers were born. Lager really is life in these countries.

While the Czechs are lager mad, the German brewing scene is also peppered with a few ales. From Berlin to Bavaria, the landscape of German beer is quite varied!

Find a seat at your neighborhood tree-lined beer garden as we explore these wonderful brewing cultures.

Kölsch

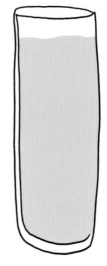

A kölsch is a beer fermented colder than normal ales and then lagered. A speciality of Cologne in Germany and served by waiters carrying trays or "kranz" full of beers.

Aroma/Flavor

Pear

Floral

Cracker

Herbal

Food Pairings:
Salad
BBQ chicken

Ingredients

Alcohol Content:
Low/Medium
Color:
Yellow to Gold
Bitterness:
Low/Medium

German hops

Pilsner malt

German
ale yeast

Altbier

Altbiers are from the city of Düsseldorf in western Germany. They are made with ale yeast but matured in lager tanks.

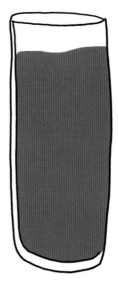

Food Pairings:
Bratwurst
Pork loin

Aroma/Flavor

Cherry

Floral

Baked bread

Herbal

Ingredients

German hops

Pilsner and Munich malts

German ale yeast

Alcohol Content:
Low/Medium
Color:
Amber to Brown
Bitterness:
Medium/High

Munich Helles

The most popular beer style in Munich! Helles is a real malt show.

Food Pairings:
Bratwurst
Ramen

Aroma/Flavor

Cracker

Grainy

Bread dough

Floral

Ingredients

German hops

Pilsner malt

Lager yeast

Alcohol Content:
Low/Medium
Color:
Yellow to Gold
Bitterness:
Low

German Pilsner

Drier and lighter than Bohemian Pilsner. A great everyday drinker and popular around the world, especially in its home country of Germany. Pairs great with sporting events.

Aroma/Flavor

 Bread dough

 Herbal

 Floral

 Cracker

Food Pairings:
Bratwurst
Pretzel

Ingredients

Alcohol Content:
Low/Medium
Color:
Yellow to Gold
Bitterness:
Medium

German hops

Pilsner malt

Lager yeast

Gose (GOH-zeh)

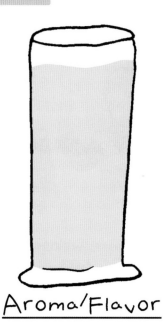

Gose is a tart ale brewed with salt and coriander. This style is associated with the German cities of Leipzig and Goslar.

Aroma/Flavor

Lemon

Sourdough

Salt

Coriander

Food Pairings:
Bagel with lox
Goat cheese

Ingredients

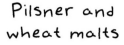
German hops

Pilsner and wheat malts

Ale yeast and Lactobacillus

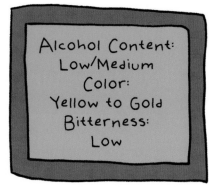

Alcohol Content:
Low/Medium
Color:
Yellow to Gold
Bitterness:
Low

Berliner Weisse

Berliner Weisse is a low-ABV tart ale from Berlin. Napoleon's troops called it the "Champagne of the North."

Aroma/Flavor

Bread dough   Lemon

Green apple   Sourdough

Food Pairings:
Goat cheese
Eggs Benedict

Ingredients

 German hops

Pilsner and wheat malt

 Ale yeast and Lactobacillus, sometimes Brettanomyces

Alcohol Content:
Low
Color:
Yellow to Gold
Bitterness:
Low

Hefeweizen or Weissbier

Hefeweizens are German ales with loads of banana and clove character. Perfect for summer evenings in a beer garden.

Aroma/Flavor

Bread dough

Banana

Bubble gum

Clove

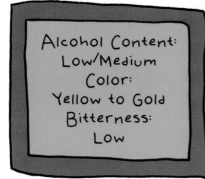

Food Pairings:
Eggs Benedict
Weisswurst

Ingredients

German hops

Pilsner and wheat malts

Hefeweizen ale yeast

Alcohol Content:
Low/Medium
Color:
Yellow to Gold
Bitterness:
Low

Dunkelweizen

Dunkelweizens are like hefeweizens but they are dark (dunkel is "dark" in German). Still refreshing and highly carbonated—reminds me of liquid banana bread!

Food Pairings:
Pancakes
Pretzel

Aroma/Flavor

Caramel

Banana

Clove

Bubble gum

Alcohol Content:
Low/Medium
Color:
Amber to Brown
Bitterness:
Low

Ingredients

German hops

Wheat, Munich, and caramel malts

Hefeweizen
ale yeast

Munich Dunkel

Munich Dunkel was the original popular beer of Munich before helles took its place. Dark and satisfying; great after a day of skiing the Bavarian Alps.

Aroma/Flavor

Walnut

Dark toast

Chocolate

Herbal

Food Pairings:
Bratwurst
Brownies

Ingredients

German hops

Munich malt

Lager yeast

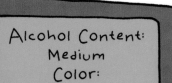

Alcohol Content:
Medium
Color:
Brown
Bitterness:
Low

Schwarzbier

Don't let the dark color fool you, schwarzbiers, also called black Pilsners, are refreshing and delicious all year long.

Aroma/Flavor

Coffee

Dark toast

Herbal

Chocolate

Food Pairings:
Roast chicken
Burrito

Ingredients

German hops

Pilsner, Munich, and black malts

Lager yeast

Alcohol Content:
Low/Medium
Color:
Brown to Black
Bitterness:
Low/Medium

148

Rauchbier

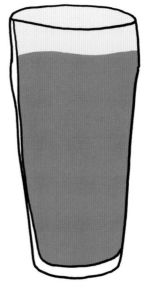

Traditional rauchbiers are smoked Märzens and come from the beautiful city of Bamberg, Germany.

Aroma/Flavor

Campfire

Bacon

Dark toast

Earthy

Food Pairings:
BBQ chicken
Prime rib

Ingredients

German hops

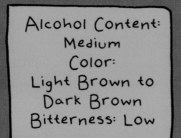

Alcohol Content:
Medium
Color:
Light Brown to
Dark Brown
Bitterness: Low

Beechwood-smoked
malt

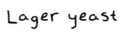
Lager yeast

Maibock

Bocks are higher-ABV lagers. Many bock labels have a goat on them, which is a symbol for fertility and rebirth. Bocks are associated with the coming of spring.

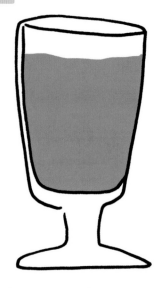

Food Pairings:
Pork loin
Bread pudding

Alcohol Content:
Medium
Color:
Golden
Bitterness:
Medium

Aroma/Flavor

Graham cracker

Toast

Earthy

Caramel

Ingredients

German hops

Pale and Munich malts

Lager yeast

Eisbock

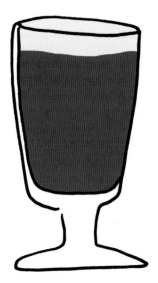

The strongest lager, eisbock is made by freezing strong bocks and removing the ice, which concentrates the beer. It's the crossroads of beer and distilling.

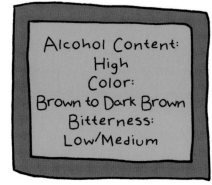

Food Pairings:
Caramel custard
Crème brûlée

Alcohol Content:
High
Color:
Brown to Dark Brown
Bitterness:
Low/Medium

Aroma/Flavor

Raisin

Toffee

Alcohol

Caramel

Ingredients

German hops

Munich malt

Lager yeast

Weizenbock

The only bock-style beer that is an ale, weizenbocks can be either pale or dark in color and vary in strength.

Food Pairings:
Banana pancakes
Lamb chops

Aroma/Flavor

Baked bread

Banana

Toast

Clove

Alcohol Content:
Medium/High
Color:
Yellow to
Dark Brown
Bitterness: Low

Ingredients

German hops

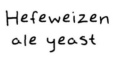
Wheat, Vienna, Munich and caramel malts

Hefeweizen ale yeast

Oktoberfest/Festbier

The modern beer of Munich's Oktoberfest celebration. Drinkable, golden in color, and served by the liter.

Aroma/Flavor

Cracker

Grainy

Bread dough

Floral

Food Pairings:
Bratwurst
Pretzel

Ingredients

German hops

Pale malts

Lager yeast

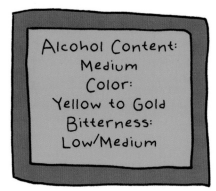

Alcohol Content:
Medium
Color:
Yellow to Gold
Bitterness:
Low/Medium

Märzen

When America thinks of "Oktoberfest" beer, they think Märzen. When it hits the shelves, it announces the start of fall.

Food Pairings:
Tacos
Bratwurst

Aroma/Flavor

Bread

Toast

Grainy

Floral

Ingredients

German hops

Pilsner and Munich malts

Lager yeast

Alcohol Content:
Medium
Color:
Gold to Amber
Bitterness:
Medium

Kellerbier or Zwickelbier

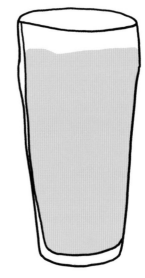

Usually an unfiltered, young lager served in summertime on draft in the beer garden. In Munich, kellerbiers are unfiltered Helles lagers.

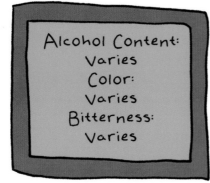

Food Pairings:
Chicken sandwich
Hot dog

Alcohol Content:
Varies
Color:
Varies
Bitterness:
Varies

Aroma/Flavor

Bread

Green apple

Grainy

Pear

Ingredients

German hops

Pale, Vienna, or
Munich malts

Lager yeast

Doppelbock

Doppelbocks were drunk for sustenance in German monasteries during the fasting season of Lent.

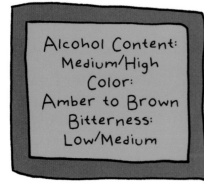

Food Pairings:
Pork loin
Jambalaya

Alcohol Content:
Medium/High
Color:
Amber to Brown
Bitterness:
Low/Medium

Aroma/Flavor

Toffee   Raisin

Dark toast   Earthy

Ingredients

 German hops

 Pale and Munich malts

 Lager yeast

Bohemian Pilsner

Bohemian Pilsners are the original Pilsners. They were created in what is now the Czech Republic by the brewery now known as Pilsner Urquell.

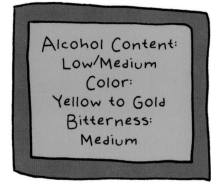

Food Pairings:
Pizza
Roast chicken

Aroma/Flavor

Spicy

Floral

Bread

Cracker

Ingredients

Alcohol Content:
Low/Medium
Color:
Yellow to Gold
Bitterness:
Medium

Czech hops

Pilsner malt

Lager yeast

Czech Amber Lager

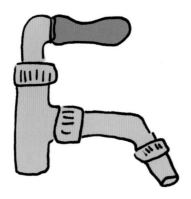

Czech amber lagers are called polotmavý, or "half dark," in their home country of the Czech Republic.

Aroma/Flavor

Graham cracker

Herbal

Toffee

Dark toast

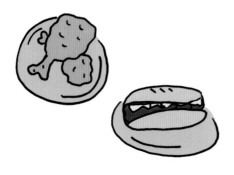

Food Pairings:
Fried chicken
Meatball sub

Ingredients

Czech hops

Pale and caramel malts

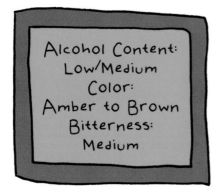

Alcohol Content:
Low/Medium
Color:
Amber to Brown
Bitterness:
Medium

Lager yeast

Czech Dark Lager

Czech dark lagers are the original lagers of the Czech Republic, being made at places such as U Fleků since 1499.

Aroma/Flavor

Molasses

Coffee

Chocolate

Dark toast

Food Pairings:
Pork tenderloin
Brownies

Ingredients

Czech hops

Pale, caramel, and chocolate malts

Lager yeast

Alcohol Content:
Low/Medium
Color:
Brown to Black
Bitterness:
Low

The United States

Ever since the Pilgrims landed in America, beer has been important to Americans.

Using tools of the trade from European brewing traditions, the U.S. beer scene has flourished and come into its own in the past 40 years.

Grab a can from the fridge, get the grill ready, and let's explore the wide and varied world of American beer styles.

American Brown Ale

Similar to English brown ales but with American ingredients, higher hopping rates, and a higher ABV. Pete's Wicked Ale was one of the first U.S. brown ales to make the big time.

Food Pairings:
Bean burrito
Fried chicken

Alcohol Content:
Low-Medium
Color:
Brown
Bitterness:
Medium

Aroma/Flavor

 Walnut

 Dark toast

 Chocolate

 Citrus

Ingredients

 American hops

 Pale, caramel, and chocolate malts

 U.S. ale yeast

Robust Porter

Robust porters are dark and satisfying—a perfect complement to the cool days of fall (or any day really).

Aroma/Flavor

Food Pairings:
Chocolate cake
Eggs Benedict

 Floral

 Coffee

 Chocolate

 Earthy

Ingredients

Alcohol Content:
Low-Medium
Color:
Brown to Black
Bitterness:
Medium

 U.S. or U.K. hops

 Pale, Munich, caramel, chocolate, and black malts

 U.S. ale yeast

American Stout

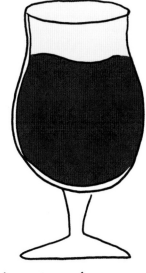

American stouts are more assertive and higher ABV than their English counterparts. A wonderful beer for winter!

Food Pairings:
Brownies
BBQ ribs

Aroma/Flavor

Grapefruit

Coffee

Chocolate

Pine

Alcohol Content:
Medium
Color:
Brown to Black
Bitterness:
Med/High

Ingredients

American hops

Pale, Munich, caramel, chocolate, and black malts

U.S. ale yeast

American Pale Ale

American pale ales are wonderful for the great outdoors like camping or hiking! Lower ABV and less hoppiness than an IPA. Think of them as IPA's little sister.

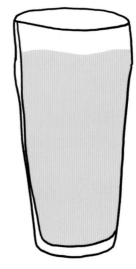

Food Pairings:
Veggie burger
Mild cheddar

Aroma/Flavor

Pine

Cracker

Grapefruit

Tropical

Ingredients

U.S. or other New World hops

Pale malts

U.S. ale yeast

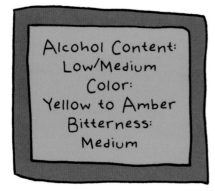

Alcohol Content:
Low/Medium
Color:
Yellow to Amber
Bitterness:
Medium

American India Pale Ale

American IPAs are as American and as popular as apple pie. Created in the 1970s, the American IPA is drinkable, usually quite bitter, and usually clear.

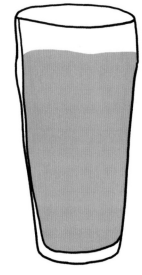

Aroma/Flavor

Food Pairings:
Tacos
Chicken sandwich

Grapefruit   Pine

Tropical   Dank

Ingredients

Alcohol Content:
Medium
Color:
Yellow to Amber
Bitterness:
High

 U.S. or other New World hops

 Pale malt plus maybe restrained use of caramel malts

 U.S. ale yeast

Juicy or Hazy India Pale Ale

An IPA style that gained popularity in the northeastern part of the U.S. Hazy and less bitter than American IPA.

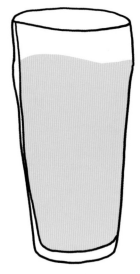

Food Pairings:
Tacos
Chocolate chip cookies

Alcohol Content:
Medium/High
Color:
Yellow to Golden
Bitterness:
Medium

Aroma/Flavor

Juicy

Tropical

Dank

Melon

Ingredients

American or other New World hops

Pale and wheat malts plus oats

U.S. or U.K. ale yeast

Double India Pale Ale

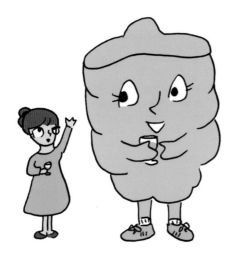

Double IPAs are the most bitter of any beer style. It's a "BIG" IPA meaning more alcohol, more hops, more of everything!

Food Pairings:
Blue cheese
Carrot cake

Alcohol Content:
High
Color:
Yellow to Amber
Bitterness:
High

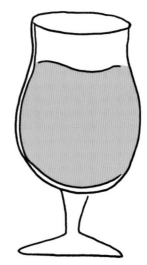

Aroma/Flavor

Grapefruit

Pine

Tropical

Dank

Ingredients

U.S. or other New World hops

Pale malts and maybe restrained use of caramel malts

U.S. ale yeast

Other IPAs

IPAs come in all strengths, flavors, and colors! Here are some IPA variants to seek out:

Brett

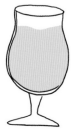

An IPA with Brettanomyces added. Creates a dry, fruity flavor with slight funk.

Black

Made with debittered black malt and piney/citrus American hops.

Session

An IPA that's under 5% ABV. Can be any color and use any hop variety.

Milkshake

An IPA with lactose added for a fuller mouthfeel—like drinking a creamsicle!

White

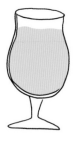

Uses Belgian witbier ale yeast and sometimes spices. Quite drinkable!

India Pale Lager

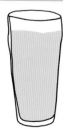

A lager hopped like an IPA. Lager yeast lets hop varieties shine.

Triple

Bigger than a Double IPA with lots of hops. A BIG BEER!

Cream Ale

Cream ale is a beer style from Western New York and Ohio. It is as refreshing and sessionable as an American lager. No one really knows why it's called a cream ale; it does not contain any milk products.

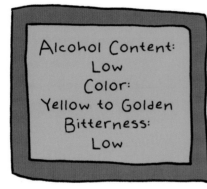

Food Pairings:
BLT
Hamburger

Alcohol Content:
Low
Color:
Yellow to Golden
Bitterness:
Low

Aroma/Flavor

Cracker

Corn

Pear

Bread dough

Ingredients

American hops

Pale malts plus flaked corn

U.S. ale or lager yeast

California Common

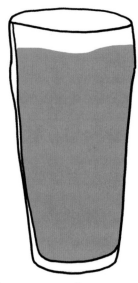

A California original made with warm-fermenting lager yeast. The modern interpretation of the style was created by San Francisco-based Anchor Brewing.

Food Pairings:
Pad thai
Pork loin

Aroma/Flavor

Graham cracker

Herbal

Pear

Toast

Ingredients

Northern Brewer hop variety

Pale, Munich, and caramel malts

California lager yeast

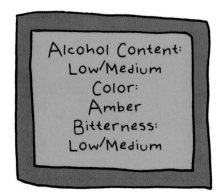
Alcohol Content:
Low/Medium
Color:
Amber
Bitterness:
Low/Medium

American Light Lager

American light lagers are the most popular lagers in America. Utterly refreshing and drinkable—the perfect complement to your summer BBQs.

Food Pairings:
Sushi
Hamburger

Alcohol Content:
Low
Color:
Yellow
Bitterness:
Low

Aroma/Flavor

Green apple

Corn

Pear

Bread dough

Ingredients

American or Continental hops

Pale malt plus corn or rice

Lager yeast

American Pilsner

Created by German immigrants using American ingredients like corn, rice and six-row barley. Made popular in the beer halls of the late 19th century.

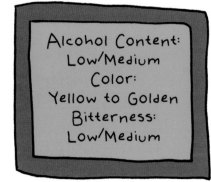

Food Pairings:
Hot dog
Salad

Alcohol Content:
Low/Medium
Color:
Yellow to Golden
Bitterness:
Low/Medium

Aroma/Flavor

Corn

Herbal

Floral

Grainy

Ingredients

American hops

Pale malt plus corn and/or rice

Lager yeast

American Wheat Beer

A beer created during the 1980s. Unlike German wheat beers, there are no banana or clove flavors.

Food Pairings:
Fried chicken
Veggie burger

Aroma/Flavor

Cracker

Grapefruit

Bread dough

Pear

Ingredients

American hops

Pale and wheat malts

U.S. ale or lager yeast

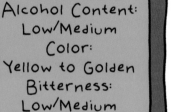

Alcohol Content:
Low/Medium
Color:
Yellow to Golden
Bitterness:
Low/Medium

American Amber/Red Ale

American amber/red ales place the emphasis on a lovely balance between malt and hop.

Aroma/Flavor

Caramel

Pine

Grapefruit

Graham cracker

Food Pairing:
Buffalo wings
Veggie quiche

Ingredients

American hops

Pale and caramel malts

U.S. ale yeast

Alcohol Content:
Low/Medium
Color:
Amber
Bitterness:
Medium

American Barleywine

One of the strongest ales, American barleywine focuses more on hop bitterness than its English counterpart. Its high ABV makes it a great holiday sipper.

Aroma/Flavor

Graham cracker

Honey

Pine

Alcohol warmth

Food Pairings:
Mushroom tart
Stilton cheese

Ingredients

U.S. hops

Pale, Vienna, and caramel malts

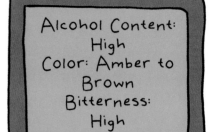

Alcohol Content: High
Color: Amber to Brown
Bitterness: High

Ale yeast

The World of Beer

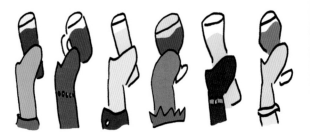

Many other countries have unique and vibrant beer cultures with interesting styles.

From Poland to Australia and beyond, beer is a shared language that the world loves.

Dry, sessionable, crisp, and tropical.

Australian Pale Ale

Popular in Poland and Russia. A big beer!

Baltic Porter

Polish style made with oak-smoked wheat malt. Highly carbonated.

Grodziskie

Mass-market lager found across the globe.

International Pale Lager

From Finland. Made with juniper and rye.

Sahti

Similar to a Märzen. Not made much now in its native Austria.

Vienna Lager

Just because they don't get their own intros doesn't diminish these styles. All beer is important!

Innovative Beer Flavors

Beer can be flavored in a lot of different ways, usually by adding ingredients to base styles to make new creations.

Mmm... chocolate!

Some delicious beer flavor examples are...

Spices

-Rosemary saison
-Lavender blonde ale
-Anise stout

Fruit

-Raspberry lambic
-Grapefruit IPA
-Apricot Gose

Sweets

-Chocolate milk stout
-Peppermint stout
-Peanut butter porter

Pumpkin

-Pumpkin porter
-Pumpkin amber ale
-Pumpkin barleywine

Coffee

I ♥ BEER

-Coffee stout
-Coffee blonde ale
-Coffee IPA

Etc.

Chicken? Money? It's happening. Experimenting with beer is fun!

How to Enjoy
Beer to the Fullest!

Glassware

Glassware has many historical and functional purposes going back centuries.

Tops on steins kept bugs and other intruders out!

Every style has correct glassware. It even makes the beer taste better.

Glassware also shows off the aesthetics of beer. Beer is beautiful!

From small snifters to big liter mugs, glassware is varied and fun.

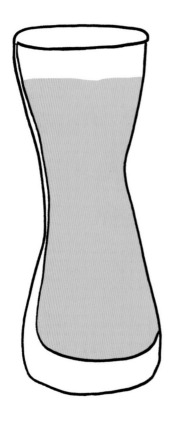

Vase

The opening at the top is large to allow for a generous head. Vase glassware is beautiful—I also use them for flowers! The size allows for a half liter (16.9 U.S. oz.) of beer. For German wheat beers like hefeweizen and dunkelweizen.

Stange

Used for Kölsch (6.75 oz.) or altbier (10-12 oz.), stange lis the German word for "stick." The small Kölsch glass is meant for quick drinking while the beer is still relatively cold.

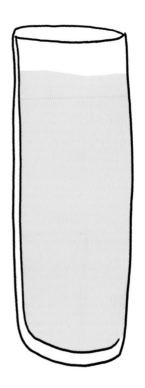

Chalice

Chalice glassware is used for Trappist and other Belgian beers. A showy glass that's part class, part marketing, and all Belgium. Many breweries have their own designs. Belgians are mad for proper glassware and take it to extremes (in the best way).

Nonic

Nonic is shorthand for "no nick"—designed to be durable and also be easy to hold for stand up drinking sessions at the pub. For session British styles like bitters and dark milds. In the U.K. and Ireland, a pint is larger than in America at around 19 U.S. oz.

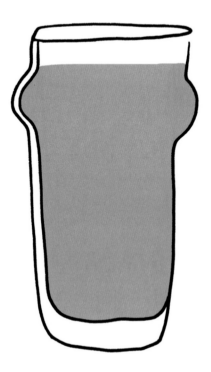

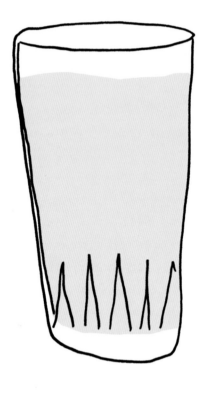

Tumbler

Used for Belgian lambics and gueuze. There's something about it that just feels like summer when you drink out of an easy-to-hold tumbler. It's a versatile glass with wide straight sides and a large mouth.

Irish Tulip

Irish tulip is a pint glass designed in the 20th century. Usually used for Irish red ales and Irish stouts but can also be used for English ales as well. Wide mouth allows you to get your nose in there.

Thistle

A glass for Scotch ales in the shape of a thistle—one of the symbols of Scotland. Can come in a variety of sizes.

Snifter

Originally for liqueurs like brandy, this glass is great for high-ABV beers such as imperial stouts and barleywines. The inward taper concentrates aroma. Good for swirling and feeling fancy on snowbound winter evenings in front of a roaring fire.

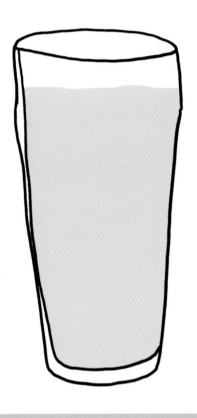

Willi Becher

The utilitarian glass of Germany (and one of my personal favorites). Great for lagers, session beers and usually half-liter sized. It has a subtle taper to hold aromas in and also makes it easy to grip.

Masskrug

Usually made in half-liter or liter sizes. Molded circles in the glass were added to show off the technology of glassmaking in the 19th century. A common sight at Oktoberfest celebrations and used in Munich, Germany year-round.

Pokal

A smaller glass for serving higher-alcohol lagers like bocks. Became associated with bocks in the 19th century but can be great for any high-ABV beer. It has a short stem to keep hands away from the beer so your body temperature doesn't warm up the beer.

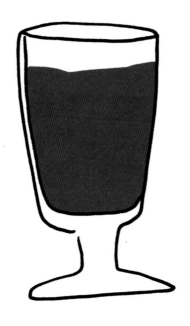

Pilsner

A beautiful tapered glass designed to show off the brilliant beauty of beers. The outward taper shows off the lovely foam as well. Not just for Pilsners though—great for schwarzbiers too!

How to Clean Glassware

Have you ever seen a dirty beer glass, those bubbles clinging to the sides? That means it's DIRTY!

Those tiny bubbles are caused by leftover fat/oil on the glass. Yuck!

Hand-washing your glassware is best. Give them a good scrub with warm/hot water and soap.

Let them air dry by using a drying rack or on a mat where air can circulate around.

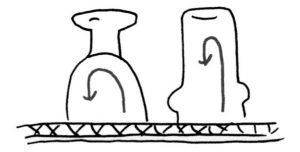

There's nothing like a beautiful beer in a clean, well cared for glass!

Know Your Beer Slang!

There's lots of beer slang out there—know what people are talking about!

Mule

Someone you bring to a beer release to buy for you if there's a max of bottles you can have. Grandmule is when you bring your grandparents.

Whale

A hard to find beer, taken from Herman Melville's famous novel, "Moby Dick." A White Whale is an extremely rare beer.

Pastry stout

A beer that mimics pastry flavors like donuts or desserts. Sometimes they are even made with those foods!

Crispy

Referring to a usually golden/pale lager. Someone who loves lagers is a "crispy kid," a.k.a me.

Bottle share

A gathering where everyone brings a beer to share. It's like a potluck, but instead of food you bring beer!

Nice haul!

Nice haul!

Thanks!

When someone remarks on the beers you have acquired. Always a good compliment to bestow.

Beer tower

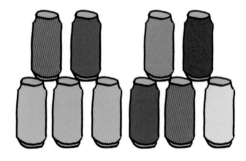

Taking a photo of beers you bought in a tower position. Makes for a nice presentation (and can make your friends jealous).

Collab

Short for "collaboration," when two breweries join forces and brew a beer together. It shows a sense of community in the beer world.

DDH

Short for "double dry hop"—when you dry hop a beer in the fermentor two times. Popular with IPAs.

Gusher

When a beer gushes when opened. This can mean a sign of infection, improperly cooled beer, or active yeast.

Cellar

Sometimes not a literal cellar, just a dark, cooler place to store your beers. Nothing like pulling a beer you've been saving in the cellar to drink for a special occasion or anytime.

Proxy

Thanks!

When someone picks up your beer order. Always nice to have someone pick up beer if you're busy.

Ticker

BEER FEST!

Someone who has to mark off every beer they drink on social media. If you go to a beer fest and see someone laboring on their phone you can assume that's what they are doing.

Dank

Since hops are related to cannabis, many can have marijuana aromas/flavors, which are usually termed "dank."

Use slang in a sentence

Be my proxy and snag me that dank whale from Vermont?

Bring them to the share and show off your haul!

Tasting Room Tips and Tricks!

Visiting a brewery's tasting room is one of life's great joys. I love going to breweries, trying their beers, and enjoying a leisurely time with friends.

Maximize your time by following some advice:

Try before you buy (not ALL of them)—asking for a sip is a great way to see if it's something you enjoy.

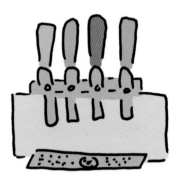

If you have a question, ask the "beertender" on staff. They've been trained to know the answers and are happy to help.

A great way of trying a brewery's offerings is by ordering smaller pours or a sampler flight tray.

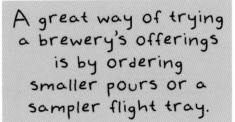

Get chatty. If the people at your table are into it, strike up a conversation. Who knows? You may meet your new best friend!

Take a tour! Lots of breweries offer tours that are either free or very affordable. Tours usually last about an hour and are a very entertaining way to learn about beer.

Have fun! Visiting a tasting room is about trying a brewery, seeing what they do, and enjoying the surroundings.

Visiting the Beer Shop

Take a trip to your local beer shop. A great place to find new brews.

Look for a packaged on/best by (BB) date when purchasing beers. Hoppy beers should be fresh.

Dates can be on neck

BB 3/4/22

On the bottom of cans →

3/4/22

On the label itself

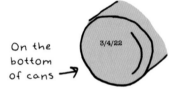

IPA

3/4/22

Shop from the cooler—beer stays fresher longer when kept cold.

Love you

Ask the clerk! They can give good suggestions and advice.

Beer Storage Tips

I like to think of beer like salad. Do you want a fresh, crisp salad or a warm, old salad? Obviously fresh!

Bottles and cans should stay upright.

This allows oxygen to stay at the top and not touch a lot of the beer.

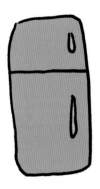

Keep most beers stored in the refrigerator if you can. Beer will stay fresher longer.

If storing outside a fridge, keep in a cool, dark place like a dry basement or closet.

Beer Travel

The world of beer is so massive! What a joy to behold.

We are lucky that anywhere we go nowadays, good beer will be waiting for us when we arrive. Good beer is everywhere!

When traveling, visit a beer festival or spend a weekend in your nearest big city.

beer!
stouts

beer!
sours

beer!
European classics

Any place you visit, there will be new beer to try. Truly the best news we've ever heard!

Hosting Your Own Tasting

Hosting your own tasting is fun and educational; invite some friends over and try it!

Have enough clean glasses for everyone and dump buckets. Don't like a beer or trying to moderate your drinking? Dump it!

Drink the beers from lightest in flavor to heaviest. Have crackers and water for everyone as a palate cleanser.

Me too.

I get pine!

Same!

Talk about each beer. What did you like or not like? It's a great way to find new beer styles!

The Beer Journey Never Ends

It's been fun but our journey here is now coming to an end.

Visit your local library to find great beer books and keep trying beers. Explore everything beer has to offer.

Most important of all is to keep an open mind. Beer is so vast—enjoy it! Cheers!

Acknowledgments

This book couldn't have been done without the support of many people. Thanks to Kristi Switzer and the crew over at Brewers Publications for believing in Visual Beer Education and to Bryan Roth and the North American Guild of Beer Writers for sending out a call for submissions to Brewers Publications. It truly is a dream come true to do a book for BP.

Thanks to fact checkers Martyn Cornell, Evan Rail, Ron Pattinson, Rob Clough, Hop Growers of America, Boak and Bailey, and the crew of Advanced Cicerone/BJCP National Judge Max Finnance, Advanced Cicerone Robyn Reid, and Master Cicerone Shane McNamara. More thanks goes to the following beer people for guidance and/or good writing: John Holl, Matthew Curtis, Chris Shephard, Maureen Ogle, Stan Hieronymus, Fox Farm Brewery, Dr. J. Nikol Jackson-Beckham, Don Tse, Lew Bryson, Kate Bernot, Jeff Alworth, Keith Villa, Randy Mosher, Mitch Steele, Patrick McGovern, and Ray Daniels.

And to beer social media and the Pints and Panels Patreon, who believe in and support P&P. Your kind words and optimism are a huge reason why Pints and Panels is successful.

Lastly, to my family (especially the goons). You deal with me talking about beer a LOT with good humor. I really, really appreciate that.

Bibliography

Brewers Association. "2021 Brewers Association Beer Style Guidelines." Accessed February 23, 2021. https://www.brewersassociation.org/edu/brewers-association-beer-style-guidelines/.

Cornell, Martyn. "A Short History of Bottled Beer." Zythophile, January 15, 2010. https://zythophile.co.uk/2010/01/15/a-short-history-of-bottled-beer/.

"Crisp Malting Group - the Process of Making Barley into Malt." YouTube, May 18, 2016. https://www.youtube.com/watch?v=nzoV375pNSM.

"Emil C. Hansen." Carlsberg, https://www.carlsberg.com/pioneers/emil-c-hansen/

Goldfarb, Aaron. "Nice Haul! the Definitive Craft Beer Urban Dictionary." VinePair, May 7, 2021. https://vinepair.com/articles/beer-geek-dictionary/.

Hieronymus, Stan. For the Love of Hops. Boulder, CO: Brewers Publications, 2012.

Mallett, John. Malt: A Practical Guide from Field to Brewhouse. Boulder, CO: Brewers Publications, 2014.

McGovern, Patrick E. Uncorking the Past: The Quest for Wine, Beer, and Other Alcoholic Beverages. Berkeley, CA: University of California Press, 2010.

Milk The Funk Wiki. "Mixed Fermentation." Last modified October 21, 2021, 15:26. http://www.milkthefunk.com/wiki/Mixed_Fermentation.

Mosher, Randy. Tasting Beer: An Insider's Guide to the World's Greatest Drink. North Adams, MA: Storey Publishing, 2017.

Oliver, Garrett. The Brewmaster's Table. New York, NY: Ecco, 2003.

Oliver, Garrett. The Oxford Companion to Beer. Oxford University Press, 2012.

Palmer, John. How to Brew: Everything You Need to Know to Brew Great Beer Every Time. Boulder, CO: Brewers Publications, 2017.

Rail, Evan. "If You Know, You Know - the Secret Handshake of Side-Pull Taps." Good Beer Hunting, March 29, 2019. https://www.goodbeerhunting.com/blog/2018/8/21/on-the-pull-czech-side-pull-taps.

Steele, Mitch. IPA Brewing Techniques, Recipes and the Evolution of India Pale Ale. Boulder, CO: Brewers Publications, 2013.

Strong, Gordon, and Kristen England. "2015 BJCP Guidelines ." BJCP guidlines , 2015. https://www.bjcp.org/docs/2015_Guidelines_Beer.pdf.

"The Temptation of the Gin Palace Door, 1844." Boak & Bailey's Beer Blog, July 4, 2020. https://boakandbailey.com/2020/03/the-temptation-of-the-gin-palace-door-1844/.

Villa, Keith. Brewing with Cannabis: Using THC and CBD in Beer. Boulder, CO: Brewers Publications, 2021.